Data Science and Machine Learning Demystified

Mastering Data Science and Machine Learning:
Advanced Techniques and Applications

Liam Stone

© Copyright 2023 - All rights reserved.

The content contained within this book may not be reproduced, duplicated or transmitted without direct written permission from the author or the publisher.

Under no circumstances will any blame or legal responsibility be held against the publisher, or author, for any damages, reparation, or monetary loss due to the information contained within this book, either directly or indirectly.

Legal Notice:

This book is copyright protected. It is only for personal use. You cannot amend, distribute, sell, use, quote or paraphrase any part, or the content within this book, without the consent of the author or publisher.

Disclaimer Notice:

Please note the information contained within this document is for educational and entertainment purposes only. All effort has been executed to present accurate, up to date, reliable, complete information. No warranties of any kind are declared or implied. Readers acknowledge that the author is not engaging in the rendering of legal, financial, medical or professional advice. The content within this book has been derived from various sources. Please consult a licensed professional before attempting any techniques outlined in this book.

By reading this document, the reader agrees that under no circumstances is the author responsible for any losses, direct or indirect, that are incurred as a result of the use of information contained within this document, including, but not limited to, errors, omissions, or inaccuracies.

Table of Contents

INTRODUCTION

The union of data science and machine learning has become a powerful force, transforming industries and altering how we interact with the outside world in an era characterized by data-driven decision-making. Welcome to "Data Science and Machine Learning Demystified: Mastering Data Science and Machine Learning - Advanced Techniques and Applications." This extensive e-book takes you on a journey into the depths of innovative techniques, revealing the complex web that unites machine learning and data science in their most potent forms.

There has never been a greater pressing need for advanced tools and strategies to extract useful insights from the massive volumes of data that are flooding around the world. This e-book is intended to serve as your guide through this complicated environment, giving you the information and abilities needed to take on challenging data problems head-on.

We recognize that you are not a newcomer to the field of machine learning and data science. You've already experienced success with simple models and understood the fundamentals. But the goal of this e-book is not to only scratch the surface; rather, it is to delve further, discover new ground, and fully utilize these technologies. In the upcoming chapters, we will explore areas where sophisticated data preprocessing methods establish the groundwork for reliable studies. We will uncover a wealth of innovative machine learning algorithms that surpass the norm and elevate your models to unprecedented levels. We'll explore the fields of deep learning and neural networks to uncover the mysteries underlying the most advanced text, picture, and sequence analysis available today. Its intricacy will be revealed through natural language processing (NLP), which will enable you to understand and successfully complete challenging language-based activities.

However, this e-book goes beyond theory. We'll explore the field of computer vision, which enables robots to comprehend visual input, and go through the challenges of time series data analysis for precise forecasting. You will learn about the nuances of unsupervised learning and clustering, which will help you find patterns in unlabeled data as well.

We won't pass up the opportunities that Reinforcement Learning presents in the spirit of innovation—letting machines learn via interaction is essential to building autonomous and adaptive systems. Nonetheless, development and ethical issues go hand in hand. We'll look at the ethical implications of these technologies so that you can become proficient in advanced skills in a responsible and ethical manner.

In addition to learning about the complex workings of data science and machine learning through these pages, you will also gain insight into how to use models in practical settings and deal with scaling issues. This journey is about the skill of mastering a discipline that has the ability to drive innovation, transform businesses, and impact our world—it's not just about tactics.

This e-book is your doorway to the world of advanced Data Science and Machine Learning, regardless of whether you're a seasoned professional looking to broaden your skill set or a novice with a strong desire to jump right in. Prepare to open doors into a world where models become predictive engines of creativity and data becomes insight. Together, let's go out on this adventure and become experts in the complex fabric of data science and machine learning.

CHAPTER I

Advanced Data Preprocessing Techniques

The Significance of Data Preprocessing in the Data Science Pipeline

Data, often hailed as the new oil, is the lifeblood of modern businesses and scientific endeavors. Yet, before data can fuel insights and discoveries, it must undergo a crucial transformation: data preprocessing. This preliminary stage within the data science pipeline is often compared to laying a sturdy foundation for a building; without it, the structure becomes unstable. In this section, we explore the profound significance of data preprocessing in the data science pipeline, shedding light on why this seemingly mundane step holds the key to extracting meaningful insights and driving successful analyses.

At the heart of data preprocessing lies the goal of improving data quality. Raw data is rarely pristine—it's riddled with imperfections, inconsistencies, and noise. These imperfections can propagate through subsequent analyses without proper handling, leading to erroneous conclusions and decisions. Data preprocessing tackles this head-on, acting as a filter that removes or rectifies anomalies, thus ensuring the integrity of downstream results. Data preprocessing fortifies the reliability of subsequent analyses by identifying and addressing missing values, outliers, and inconsistencies.

Beyond mere data quality enhancement, data preprocessing significantly impacts the efficiency of the analysis process. In today's fast-paced world, time is of the essence, and data scientists cannot afford to be bogged down by sluggish computations. Preprocessing steps such as dimensionality reduction, where irrelevant or redundant features are eliminated, enhance model performance and expedite computation. This is particularly crucial in scenarios involving vast datasets or real-time applications, where efficiency can differentiate between actionable insights and missed opportunities.

Data preprocessing is also a realm where domain knowledge and intuition come to play. A data scientist intimately acquainted with the context of the data can make informed decisions about how to handle missing values or outliers. For instance, in medical data analysis, an outlier might signify a rare but significant occurrence. Here, removing it could obscure crucial insights. In contrast, for financial data analysis, an outlier might indicate an error or fraudulent activity, necessitating its removal. Data preprocessing bridges the gap between raw data and meaningful insights, amplifying the power of data-driven decisions.

The significance of data preprocessing extends to its pivotal role in preparing data for machine learning algorithms. Machine learning models are hungry for well-structured, normalized, and scaled data. Failure to preprocess data appropriately can lead to suboptimal model performance, rendering the efforts invested in algorithm selection and tuning futile. Feature scaling, a preprocessing step that standardizes the range of features, ensures that no single feature dominates the learning process due to differences in magnitude. Without this step, models like Support Vector Machines and k-Nearest Neighbors might struggle to converge or generalize effectively.

Moreover, data preprocessing serves as a bridge between disparate data sources. In real-world scenarios, data might be collected from various sensors, databases, or sources with varying formats and scales. These disparities can hinder analyses and lead to inaccurate insights. Preprocessing harmonizes such data, converting it into a consistent format and scale. This transformation not only simplifies subsequent analysis but also unlocks the potential for cross-domain insights that would otherwise remain concealed.

In conclusion, the significance of data preprocessing in the data science pipeline is undeniable. It transforms raw data into a refined, structured, and reliable form that underpins the entirety of the analytical process. Data preprocessing is more than just a necessary chore; it's an art that requires domain expertise, creativity, and a keen eye for detail. By purging anomalies, enhancing efficiency, facilitating machine learning, and harmonizing diverse data sources, data preprocessing lays the foundation upon which accurate insights, informed decisions, and innovative discoveries are built. Just as a painter primes their canvas before crafting a masterpiece, data scientists preprocess their data to create a foundation for brilliance in the world of data-driven exploration.

Exploring Essential Data Preprocessing Techniques: Handling Missing Data, Outlier Detection, and Feature Scaling

In the vast landscape of data science, the journey from raw data to actionable insights is paved with challenges and complexities. Data preprocessing, often described as the cornerstone of this journey, is a set of transformative techniques that can make or break the quality and reliability of subsequent analyses. In this section, we delve into three fundamental data preprocessing techniques—handling missing data, outlier detection, and feature scaling—to unravel their significance, mechanisms, and impact on the data science pipeline.

Missing data is a pervasive issue that can cast shadows of uncertainty on analyses. Whether due to measurement errors, data entry issues, or other factors, gaps in the dataset can skew results and compromise the validity of conclusions. Handling missing data is a nuanced task that involves striking a delicate balance between preserving the integrity of the dataset and avoiding the introduction of bias. There exist multiple strategies for managing missing data, ranging from simple techniques like mean imputation and forward-fill to more sophisticated methods such as regression imputation and k-nearest neighbor imputation.

The choice of strategy hinges on the nature of the data, the underlying assumptions of the analysis, and the potential impact on downstream tasks. Imputation, while effective, must be wielded with caution, as it can inadvertently introduce artificial patterns. Alternatively, when the proportion of missing data is substantial, it might be judicious to explore methods that leverage machine learning algorithms to predict and fill in missing values. Ultimately, mastering the art of handling missing data empowers data scientists to navigate this common challenge and ensure the integrity of their analyses.

Outliers, those data points that deviate significantly from the norm, have the power to influence analysis outcomes disproportionately. They can distort statistical measures, impact model accuracy, and lead to skewed insights. Outlier detection, therefore, becomes a critical step in the data preprocessing journey. The techniques employed for outlier detection aim to identify and isolate these exceptional data points for further examination.
One popular approach involves using statistical measures like the Z-score or the Interquartile Range (IQR) to identify data points that fall far from the mean or median. Another method utilizes machine learning algorithms to build models that can distinguish between normal and outlier data points. The challenge in outlier detection lies in determining the threshold beyond which a data point is deemed an outlier. Striking the right balance between capturing genuine anomalies and avoiding overfitting is a task that necessitates domain knowledge and a keen understanding of the data's context.

In the intricate dance of data features, the scales upon which they exist can greatly influence the behavior of machine learning algorithms. Feature scaling, a preprocessing technique, standardizes the range of features, ensuring that no single feature dominates the learning process due to differences in magnitude. Without feature scaling, algorithms like Support Vector Machines and k-Nearest Neighbors might struggle to converge or generalize effectively.

Two common methods of feature scaling are normalization and standardization. Normalization scales features to a common range, often between 0 and 1, while standardization transforms them to have zero mean and unit variance. The choice between these methods depends on the distribution of the data and the characteristics of the algorithm being employed. The impact of feature scaling reverberates through the entire data science pipeline, influencing not only the performance of machine learning models but also the interpretation of model coefficients and the convergence of optimization algorithms.

In conclusion, the techniques of handling missing data, outlier detection, and feature scaling stand as integral pillars within the edifice of data preprocessing. Each technique addresses a specific challenge, yet collectively, they harmonize to sculpt a dataset that is robust, reliable, and ready for analysis. As data scientists navigate the complexities of real-world data, these preprocessing techniques serve as guiding lights, illuminating the path toward accurate insights and informed decisions. By mastering the intricacies of managing missing data, identifying outliers, and scaling features, data scientists empower themselves to extract the hidden gems buried within the data, transforming raw information into actionable knowledge. In the grand symphony of data analysis, these preprocessing techniques play a symphonic role, setting the stage for the harmonious crescendo of discovery.

Introduction of advanced preprocessing techniques like dimensionality reduction

In the intricate tapestry of data science, the term "dimensionality" transcends its mathematical roots to become a defining factor that shapes the fate of analytical endeavors. As datasets burgeon in complexity and diversity, the curse of dimensionality emerges—a phenomenon where an abundance of features overwhelms the analysis process, leading to increased computational costs, overfitting, and diminished model interpretability. Enter dimensionality reduction, a transformative preprocessing technique that wields the power to distill the essence of data while preserving its intrinsic patterns. In this section, we embark on a voyage into the realm of advanced preprocessing techniques, casting a spotlight on dimensionality reduction, its methods, and its profound impact on the landscape of data science.

Richard E. Bellman's term, "the curse of dimensionality," captures the difficulties that result from data being dispersed over a large number of features. As the number of features grows, the volume of the data space increases exponentially, leading to data sparsity and computational inefficiency. Moreover, high-dimensional data tends to be susceptible to overfitting, where models capture noise rather than meaningful patterns. This phenomenon can result in poor generalization to new data, rendering analyses less reliable and predictions less accurate. The question that arises is how to navigate this complex realm while retaining the essence of the data.
Dimensionality reduction is a powerful technique that seeks to alleviate the challenges of high-dimensional data by transforming it into a lower-dimensional representation. The essence of the data—its patterns, relationships, and variations—is preserved while discarding redundant or noise-ridden features. This not only mitigates the curse of dimensionality but also enhances the interpretability of models, as lower-

dimensional spaces are more amenable to visualization and analysis.

One of the foundational methods in dimensionality reduction is Principal Component Analysis (PCA). At its core, PCA identifies the orthogonal axes—termed principal components—that capture the maximum variance in the data. By projecting the data onto these components, it's possible to create a lower-dimensional representation that retains the most significant information. PCA not only reduces dimensionality but also decorrelates features, a trait that's valuable when dealing with multicollinearity—a situation where features are correlated.

While PCA primarily focuses on preserving global structures, t-Distributed Stochastic Neighbor Embedding (or t-SNE) is a dimensionality reduction technique that specializes in capturing local patterns. t-SNE transforms high-dimensional data into a lower-dimensional space in a way that maintains the similarity relationships between data points. This makes it a potent tool for visualizing complex datasets, where clusters and groupings become vividly apparent. The ability to convert high-dimensional data into two or three dimensions while retaining meaningful distances fosters insights that might otherwise remain concealed in the high-dimensional abyss.

In the realm of deep learning, autoencoders are a fascinating dimensionality reduction technique. Autoencoders has an encoder and a decoder, which work in tandem to compress the data into a lower-dimensional latent space and then reconstruct it. While autoencoders have dimensionality reduction as a side effect, their true power lies in their ability to learn abstract representations of data. These learned representations can serve as rich features for subsequent analyses, offering a bridge between raw data and the intricate patterns hidden within.

Central to dimensionality reduction is the concept of information preservation. The challenge lies in striking a balance—reducing dimensionality while retaining the essential characteristics of the data. This entails careful consideration of the variance explained, the retained components, and the trade-offs between dimensionality reduction and the goals of analysis. While dimensionality reduction can enhance computational efficiency and model performance, it's imperative to tread cautiously, as excessive reduction can lead to loss of information and potentially misleading insights.

The impact of dimensionality reduction spans diverse domains. In fields like image processing, where each pixel is a feature, dimensionality reduction can condense the essence of an image while retaining its visual appeal. In genetics, where genes represent features, dimensionality reduction can aid in identifying patterns that characterize diseases. In natural language processing, where the dimensionality explodes with the vocabulary, techniques like word embeddings reduce words to dense, meaningful vectors.

Dimensionality reduction isn't devoid of challenges. The selection of a proper method depends on the nature of the data and the goals of analysis. Overfitting in the reduced space, the interpretability of lower-dimensional features, and the curse of interpretability—the risk of losing the ability to explain the transformed features in meaningful terms—are all considerations that require careful thought. Moreover, dimensionality reduction isn't a one-size-fits-all solution; what works well for one dataset might not be suitable for another.

In conclusion, dimensionality reduction stands as a gateway to a world where complexity is tamed, patterns are distilled, and insights are magnified. It transforms high-dimensional data into lower-dimensional representations, preserving the essence while mitigating the challenges posed by the curse of dimensionality. Whether through the lens of PCA, the vividness of t-SNE, or the power of autoencoders, dimensionality reduction is a symphony that orchestrates data's intricacies into a harmonious narrative.

As the data landscape continues to evolve, dimensionality reduction remains a beacon of insight—a technique that not only enhances computational efficiency and model performance but also kindles the flames of discovery. It's a testament to the art of data science—a delicate balance between abstraction and information preservation, between simplification and insight generation. Dimensionality reduction, in its myriad forms, empowers data scientists to navigate the labyrinthine dimensions of data, revealing the hidden stories that lie beneath the surface. In the vast sea of data science, dimensionality reduction serves as both compass and compass, guiding analyses toward clarity and understanding.

CHAPTER II

Advanced Machine Learning Algorithms

Exploring advanced machine learning algorithms beyond the basics

Once a niche pursuit, machine learning has risen to the forefront of technological innovation, reshaping industries, and revolutionizing the way we interact with data. At the heart of this transformation lie the algorithms that fuel machine learning models' predictive and analytical capabilities. While the foundational algorithms have paved the way for progress, the true potential of machine learning unfolds when we delve into the realm of advanced techniques. In this section, we embark on a journey to explore the significance and impact of advanced machine learning algorithms beyond the basics, delving into the depths of ensemble methods, support vector machines, and neural networks.

The journey of machine learning algorithms begins with the classics—linear regression, decision trees, and k-nearest neighbors. These algorithms laid the groundwork for understanding concepts such as prediction and classification. However, as data grew in complexity and quantity, the limitations of these foundational algorithms became evident. This spurred the development of advanced techniques that could tackle intricate patterns and high-dimensional data.

One of the most transformative advancements in machine learning is the concept of ensemble methods. These methods take a collaborative approach, combining the predictions of numerous models to create a more accurate and robust final prediction. Techniques like Random Forests, Gradient Boosting, and AdaBoost leverage the collective wisdom of diverse models, mitigating the shortcomings of individual algorithms. By reducing overfitting, enhancing generalization, and improving prediction accuracy, ensemble methods stand
as a testament to the synergy that emerges when algorithms collaborate.

Support Vector Machines (SVM) are a category of algorithms that have gained prominence for their prowess in high-dimensional spaces. SVMs are particularly effective for classification tasks, where they draw hyperplanes to delineate different classes while maximizing the margin between them. This ability to find optimal decision boundaries has made SVMs a staple in fields like image classification, text analysis, and bioinformatics. Moreover, the introduction of kernel functions has extended SVMs' capabilities, allowing them to uncover complex, non-linear patterns that lie hidden within the data.

The resurgence of neural networks, particularly deep neural networks, has marked a watershed moment in the field of machine learning. Inspired by the human brain's intricate architecture, neural networks simulate layers of interconnected neurons that process and transform data. A subset of machine learning that is anchored in neural networks with multiple hidden layers, capable of learning intricate hierarchies of features is known as deep learning. Convolutional Neural Networks (CNNs) have revolutionized image analysis, while Recurrent Neural

Networks (RNNs) have redefined sequence prediction tasks. The introduction of attention mechanisms, Gated Recurrent Units (GRUs), and Long Short-Term Memory (LSTM) cells has further expanded the capabilities of neural networks, enabling them to excel in tasks like machine translation, speech recognition, and more.

While the potential of advanced machine learning algorithms is undeniable, their implementation is not without challenges. Complexity and computational requirements escalate as algorithms become more sophisticated. Interpretability—the ability to understand and explain model decisions—can diminish as models become more intricate, raising ethical and transparency concerns. Overfitting, a perennial concern in machine learning, remains a challenge even with advanced algorithms, necessitating careful regularization techniques.

The impact of advanced machine learning algorithms reverberates across industries. In healthcare, they aid in disease diagnosis and prognosis prediction. In finance, they forecast market trends and manage risk. In autonomous vehicles, they power perception and decision-making. The transformative power of these algorithms lies in their ability to extract nuanced insights and make accurate predictions from intricate datasets. As we venture into the realm of advanced machine learning algorithms, a delicate balance emerges between complexity and utility. Selecting the right algorithm for a certain task demands an understanding of the problem, the data, and the trade-offs involved. While advanced algorithms promise superior performance, they also require more data and computational resources. The quest lies in discerning when the complexity is justified by the potential gain in accuracy and insights.

In conclusion, the world of machine learning is a vibrant tapestry woven with algorithms of varying complexity and capability. While the basics serve as an initiation, the true marvels of machine learning come to life when we venture beyond the surface. Ensemble methods synergize diverse models, SVMs draw hyperplanes of knowledge, and neural networks simulate the human brain's capacity to learn. The marriage of these advanced algorithms with domain knowledge and thoughtful experimentation unlocks the potential to tackle intricate patterns, make precise predictions, and unravel insights that lie hidden within the data's folds.

As we stand on the precipice of ever-evolving technological landscapes, advanced machine learning algorithms stand as our allies, equipping us to confront complex challenges and unearth opportunities that were once deemed beyond reach. This journey is a testament to the dynamism of the field—a perpetual exploration of techniques that push the boundaries of what machines can learn, comprehend, and achieve. In embracing the intricacies of advanced machine learning algorithms, we embrace the art of transforming data into knowledge and dreams into reality.

Exploring the Symphony of Ensemble Methods such as Random Forest, Gradient Boosting, and Stacking

In the ever-evolving landscape of machine learning, the pursuit of predictive accuracy and robustness has given rise to a powerful strategy: ensemble methods. These methods, akin to the wisdom of crowds, harness the collective knowledge of multiple models to create a more accurate and resilient prediction. Within this paradigm, three prominent techniques—Random Forest, Gradient

Boosting, and Stacking—stand as pillars of innovation. In this section, we dive deep into the realm of ensemble methods, uncovering their mechanics, benefits, and real-world applications.

At the heart of ensemble methods lies the belief that diverse models, when combined judiciously, can outperform any single model. Ensemble methods offer a way to mitigate the shortcomings and biases inherent in individual algorithms, creating a more robust and accurate prediction by aggregating their outputs. This approach is reminiscent of diverse experts coming together to offer their perspectives, resulting in a more informed decision.

Random Forest, an ensemble technique rooted in decision trees, exemplifies the power of collaboration. Decision trees, while interpretable, are prone to overfitting and instability. Random Forest addresses these limitations by constructing a decision trees ensemble, each trained on a subset of the data and with a subset of features. The outputs of these trees are aggregated to form a consensus prediction. By introducing randomness in the feature selection and the data used for training, Random Forest reduces overfitting and enhances the model's robustness.

Gradient Boosting, a powerful technique that has gained significant popularity, takes a different approach to ensemble learning. Instead of relying on randomness, it sequentially builds a strong model by focusing on the mistakes of its predecessors. Each new model, known as a weak learner, is trained to correct the errors made by the ensemble up to that point. This iterative process fine-tunes the model's accuracy, resulting in a predictive powerhouse. Techniques like XGBoost, LightGBM, and CatBoost have further refined Gradient Boosting, introducing optimizations that accelerate the training process and improve performance.

Stacking, also known as meta-learning, is an ensemble technique that orchestrates the collaboration of diverse models in a hierarchical manner. Instead of directly combining the outputs of base models, stacking introduces a meta-model that learns to combine their predictions based on their strengths and weaknesses. This meta-model, often referred to as a "blender" or a "meta-learner," takes the predictions of base models as inputs and learns how to weigh and integrate them optimally. Stacking's flexibility and ability to leverage the complementary capabilities of multiple models make it a potent strategy for boosting predictive performance.

The power of ensemble methods reverberates across a spectrum of industries. In finance, ensemble methods enhance the accuracy of credit scoring models and market trend predictions. In healthcare, they aid in disease diagnosis and drug discovery. In image analysis, they improve object detection and facial recognition. In each domain, the ensemble approach harmonizes diverse insights, creating a predictive symphony that outshines individual models.

While ensemble methods offer a plethora of benefits, they also come with challenges. The increased complexity of ensembles can lead to longer training times and higher computational requirements. Interpretability, a prized trait in machine learning, can diminish as the ensemble's intricacies grow. Additionally, the selection of hyperparameters and the optimization of ensemble components require thoughtful experimentation and tuning.

Choosing the right ensemble method and configuring its components is akin to orchestrating a masterpiece. The choice depends on factors like the nature of the problem, the dataset's characteristics, and the trade-offs between accuracy and interpretability. Moreover, the composition of an ensemble involves selecting diverse models that complement each other's strengths and weaknesses. While diversity is crucial, the models should also be adept at capturing different aspects of the underlying patterns.

In conclusion, ensemble methods represent a journey into the art of collaborative learning. The philosophy of combining diverse models to create a more accurate and resilient prediction reflects the essence of innovation—where the sum is greater than its parts. Random Forest harnesses the collective wisdom of decision trees, Gradient Boosting ascends the gradient of accuracy through iterative refinement, and Stacking orchestrates the harmony of meta-models. These techniques stand as testament to the dynamic nature of machine learning—a field where innovation is nurtured by collaboration.

As the landscape of data continues to evolve, ensemble methods emerge as a beacon of predictive prowess, allowing us to navigate the complexities of data with greater precision. In embracing the orchestration of multiple models, we embrace the essence of machine learning—a continuous quest to amplify our predictive capabilities and uncover insights hidden within the data. The journey into ensemble methods is a symphony of innovation—a crescendo that blends algorithms into a harmonious composition, creating predictions that resonate with accuracy and ingenuity.

Introduction of support vector machines (SVM), k-nearest neighbors (KNN), and neural networks

Machine learning algorithms are the backbone of modern data-driven decision-making, offering a window into the potential locked within vast datasets. Among the pantheon of algorithms, three hold a special place—Support Vector Machines (SVM), K-Nearest Neighbors (KNN), and Neural Networks. In this section, we delve into the intricacies of these algorithms, exploring their mechanics, strengths, and diverse applications that have transformed industries and domains.

Support Vector Machines, or SVMs, are a class of algorithms that excel in classification tasks. At their core, SVMs seek to find the optimal hyperplane that separates data points belonging to different classes while maximizing the margin between them. This hyperplane not only classifies new data points but also provides insights into the underlying patterns of the data. SVMs can also handle non-linear separations through the use of kernel functions, which transform the data into higher-dimensional spaces where linear separation becomes feasible.

The elegance of SVMs lies in their ability to focus on the most informative data points—support vectors—located on the margins or near the decision boundary. By honing in on these critical data points, SVMs reduce the risk of overfitting and generalize well to unseen data. Their versatility extends beyond binary classification to multi-class problems and even regression tasks. With applications ranging from text categorization and image recognition to biological data analysis, SVMs have carved a niche as powerful tools for data scientists seeking robust and accurate classification.

K-Nearest Neighbors, or KNN, embodies the principle that similar instances tend to share common attributes. KNN operates on the notion that an instance's neighbors—those with similar features—are indicative of its class or value. Given a new data point, KNN identifies the 'k' nearest neighbors and assigns the class (in classification) or computes the value (in regression) based on a majority or weighted vote. KNN's simplicity is its strength; it doesn't require explicit model training but instead learns from the data itself.

However, KNN does come with trade-offs. Its performance heavily relies on the selection of 'k' and the distance metric, which demand careful selection based on the problem domain. Additionally, KNN is sensitive to the curse of dimensionality, where the effectiveness of distance-based methods decreases as the number of features increases. KNN shines in applications such as recommendation systems, anomaly detection, and imputation of missing values. It finds its place in scenarios where data points' proximity carries significant predictive power.

The emergence of neural networks signifies a paradigm shift in machine learning—an approach that emulates the human brain's capacity to learn and adapt. Neural networks has layers of interconnected nodes, or neurons, that process and transform data. These networks are divided into an input layer, hidden layers that extract features, and an output layer that provides the final prediction. Deep neural networks, characterized by multiple hidden layers, excel in capturing intricate patterns, enabling applications including natural language processing (NLP), image recognition, as well as autonomous driving.

Convolutional Neural Networks (CNNs) are specialized for image analysis, using convolutional layers to identify features like edges and textures. Recurrent Neural Networks (RNNs) excel in sequences, making them suitable for tasks including speech recognition and language modeling. Long Short-Term Memory (or LSTM) networks and Gated Recurrent Units (or GRUs) address RNNs' short-term memory limitations, making them adept at capturing longer dependencies in sequential data. Neural networks, however, demand substantial data for training and extensive computational resources for optimization.

The triumvirate of SVM, KNN, and neural networks extends its influence across a spectrum of industries. SVMs excel in tasks such as sentiment analysis, text classification, and medical diagnosis. KNN's proximity-based reasoning is instrumental in collaborative filtering for recommendation systems and anomaly detection in cybersecurity. Neural networks, on the other hand, are foundational in fields like computer vision, powering facial recognition, object detection, and self-driving cars. They also shape the landscape of natural language processing, enabling chatbots, machine translation, and sentiment analysis.
While these algorithms offer remarkable capabilities, they are not devoid of challenges. SVMs' performance can be sensitive to hyperparameter tuning and the choice of kernel function. KNN's effectiveness is highly dependent on data distribution and requires preprocessing to handle feature scaling and dimensionality reduction. Neural networks demand careful architecture design, extensive data preprocessing, and can be prone to overfitting when dealing with limited data.

The selection of algorithm depends on various factors, including the nature of the problem, the volume of available data, and the trade-offs between interpretability and accuracy. SVMs are preferred when seeking a robust decision boundary, KNN when proximity carries predictive power, and neural networks when intricate patterns need capturing. The art lies in understanding the strengths and weaknesses of each algorithm and aligning them with the problem's nuances.

In conclusion, support Vector Machines, K-Nearest Neighbors, and Neural Networks encapsulate the essence of machine learning's evolution—harnessing mathematical principles, proximity-based reasoning, and the complexity of the human brain. They stand as a testament to the power of algorithms that have reshaped industries, unlocked insights, and redefined possibilities. From SVM's hyperplanes of insight to KNN's proximity-driven predictions and neural networks' intricate pattern recognition, this trio reflects the multidimensional landscape of machine learning.

As we navigate the data-rich era, these algorithms serve as guiding lights, illuminating the path toward accurate predictions, informed decisions, and transformative discoveries. Their potency lies not only in their technical capabilities but also in their capacity to unveil the hidden stories buried within data's depths. The journey into the realms of SVM, KNN, and neural networks is a journey into the heart of machine learning's innovation—a journey that unfolds as a symphony of algorithms, harmonizing insights, and shaping the future of data-driven intelligence.

CHAPTER III

Deep Learning and Neural Networks

Understanding neural networks and their architecture

In the realm of artificial intelligence, neural networks stand as a shining beacon of innovation—a testament to the human desire to emulate the intricacies of the brain's information processing. These computational marvels, fueled by layers of interconnected nodes, have revolutionized fields ranging from computer vision to natural language processing. In this section, we embark on a journey into the world of neural networks, delving into their mechanics, architectural complexities, and the transformative impact they've wielded across industries.

The inception of neural networks was inspired by the human brain—a complex network of neurons that process and transmit information through synaptic connections. This biological phenomenon served as the blueprint for artificial neural networks, where neurons are replaced by mathematical units that perform operations on input data. These units, also known as nodes or artificial neurons, interact through weighted connections, capturing the essence of information flow and transformation.

At the heart of a neural network lies its architecture, a composition of layers that govern the information transformation process. The core layers include the input layer, where data is introduced, the output layer, where predictions are generated, and intermediate hidden layers that extract hierarchical features from the input data. The architecture's depth—the number of hidden layers— defines the network's depth, a factor that influences its ability to capture intricate patterns.

Within each layer reside neurons, which are interconnected with the neurons of adjacent layers. A neuron's functionality mirrors that of its biological counterpart—it receives inputs, processes them using a weighted sum, applies an activation function to introduce non-linearity, and passes the result to the next layer. This interconnected structure allows neural networks to extract progressively complex features as data flows through the layers.

The concept of activation functions introduces a crucial non-linearity to neural networks, enabling them to model complex relationships in data. These functions are applied to the weighted sum of inputs within each neuron, determining whether the neuron should be activated or not. Popular activation functions include the sigmoid function, which compresses the output between 0 and 1, the hyperbolic tangent (tanh) function, which ranges between -1 and 1, and Rectified Linear Unit (ReLU), which outputs the input for positive values and zero for negatives.

Activation functions empower neural networks to capture non-linear patterns, paving the way for the extraction of intricate features that might be otherwise inaccessible using linear models. The choice of activation function influences the network's learning behavior, convergence speed, and resistance to vanishing gradients—a challenge where gradients diminish in earlier layers during training.

Neural networks learn through a process known as training, where they adjust their internal parameters— weights and biases—based on the input data and desired outputs. The core learning mechanisms are feedforward and backpropagation. The term "feedforward" describes how data moves from the input layer through the output layer in a network, producing predictions. These predictions are then compared with the actual targets to compute an error, also known as the loss.

Backpropagation, a cornerstone of neural network training, involves the computation of gradients that quantify how much each parameter contributed to the error. These gradients are used to update the parameters in a way that minimizes the error—usually through optimization techniques like gradient descent. The iterative interplay between feedforward and backpropagation leads to parameter adjustments that enable the network to approximate complex functions and make accurate predictions.

The advent of deep learning—a subfield of machine learning focused on neural networks with multiple hidden layers—has sparked a revolution in artificial intelligence. Deep neural networks, or deep networks, excel at capturing intricate patterns and hierarchies within data. Convolutional Neural Networks (CNNs) specialize in image analysis by using convolutional layers to detect local features like edges and textures. Recurrent Neural Networks (RNNs) thrive in sequence data, making them suitable for tasks such as speech recognition and natural language processing.

Architectural innovations have further extended neural network capabilities. Long Short-Term Memory (LSTM) cells and Gated Recurrent Units (GRUs) address RNNs' short-term memory limitations, enabling them to capture longer dependencies in sequences. Attention mechanisms enhance neural networks' ability to focus on relevant parts of input data, making them more effective in tasks like text summarization and machine translation.

While neural networks offer transformative capabilities, they come with challenges. Training deep networks demands substantial amounts of data and computational resources. Overfitting, a phenomenon where networks memorize training data rather than generalize, necessitates regularization techniques. The choice of architecture, including the number of layers and nodes, requires careful consideration based on the problem's complexity and the available data.

Interpretability poses another challenge; as neural networks grow in complexity, understanding the reasoning behind their predictions becomes more elusive. Ethical concerns also arise as neural networks influence decision-making in critical domains like healthcare and finance.

The versatility of neural networks permeates diverse industries. In healthcare, they aid in disease diagnosis, drug discovery, and personalized treatment plans. In finance, they forecast market trends, detect fraudulent activities, and manage risks. Autonomous vehicles rely on neural networks for perception and decision-making. Natural language processing powers chatbots, language translation, and sentiment analysis.

In conclusion, neural networks are the epitome of computational innovation—a testament to humanity's drive to emulate the complexity of the brain's cognitive processes. Their architectural intricacies, encompassing layers, neurons, and activation functions, orchestrate a symphony of data transformation and predictive insights.

As deep learning opens new horizons, neural networks become a canvas for capturing intricate patterns that shape industries, transform societies, and redefine the possibilities of artificial intelligence. The journey into neural networks is an expedition into the heart of intelligence—an exploration that continually pushes the boundaries of what machines can learn, comprehend, and achieve.

Explanation of the concepts of deep learning and its applications in image, text, and sequence data

In the intricate landscape of artificial intelligence, deep learning has emerged as a revolutionary force, reshaping the way machines comprehend and interpret data. Rooted in neural network architectures with multiple hidden layers, deep learning delves beyond the surface, capturing complex patterns and relationships that traditional methods struggle to unveil. In this section, we embark on an exploration of deep learning's foundational concepts and its transformative applications in image analysis, natural language processing, and sequence data manipulation.

At the heart of deep learning lies the concept of neural networks with numerous hidden layers, each layer contributing to the gradual extraction of intricate features from raw data. Unlike traditional machine learning algorithms that depend on handcrafted features, deep learning autonomously learns and refines features through a hierarchy of layers. This ability to autonomously discover relevant representations enables deep learning models to capture nuanced patterns and relationships within data, making them particularly adept at complex tasks.

Deep learning has ushered in a renaissance in computer vision, enabling machines to perceive, interpret, and understand visual data at unprecedented levels. Convolutional Neural Networks (CNNs) have emerged as the backbone of image analysis, mimicking the human visual cortex's hierarchical feature detection. CNNs use convolutional layers to detect edges, textures, and shapes, followed by pooling layers that reduce spatial dimensions while preserving essential information. The final layers translate extracted features into class probabilities or bounding boxes, allowing the network to recognize objects, segment images, and even generate art.

From medical imaging, where CNNs aid in disease diagnosis, to autonomous vehicles, where they enable object detection and lane tracking, deep learning's image analysis prowess transcends industries. Image generation, exemplified by Generative Adversarial Networks (GANs), enables the creation of realistic images, revolutionizing fields like fashion design, interior decorating, and even video game development.
In the realm of language, deep learning has orchestrated a symphony of advancements through Natural Language Processing (NLP). Recurrent Neural Networks (or RNNs) and their variants, like Long Short-Term Memory (LSTM) and Gated Recurrent Units (GRUs), excel in capturing sequential dependencies in text. This capability enables sentiment analysis, text classification, and language generation. Attention mechanisms enhance the model's focus on relevant parts of input, propelling NLP tasks like machine translation, where the complexities of languages are translated with remarkable accuracy.

Transformer architecture, introduced with models like BERT (Bidirectional Encoder Representations from

Transformers), marks another milestone in NLP. BERT's contextual understanding of words within sentences has revolutionized tasks like question answering, text completion, and named entity recognition. Language models like GPT-3 (Generative Pre-trained Transformer 3) generate coherent text, demonstrating a grasp of context, humor, and even storytelling.

Sequences—data points arranged in chronological order—are ubiquitous in various domains, from speech to genomics. Deep learning's stronghold on sequence data is showcased by its applications in speech recognition and generation. Recurrent neural networks, with their memory of past inputs, excel in speech-to-text conversion and speech synthesis. Bidirectional RNNs leverage information from both past and future inputs, enhancing their understanding of temporal patterns.

Sequence-to-sequence models have disrupted machine translation, summarization, and dialogue generation. Encoder-decoder architectures, often powered by LSTMs or Transformers, encode input sequences into a fixed-size vector representation and decode it into an output sequence. This technique allows seamless translation between languages and even generates coherent responses in chatbots.

While deep learning's accomplishments are undeniable, challenges loom on the horizon. Deep models demand substantial computational resources for training, raising concerns about energy consumption and accessibility. Overfitting remains a concern, especially in scenarios with limited data. Interpretability, a cornerstone of trustworthy AI, diminishes as networks grow in complexity, posing ethical challenges, particularly in domains like healthcare and finance.

Continual advancements, however, push the frontiers of deep learning. Self-supervised learning, where models learn from unlabeled data, offers promise in scenarios with sparse annotations. Few-shot learning, demonstrated by models like GPT-3, showcases the ability to make predictions from a handful of examples, bridging the gap between training data and real-world scenarios.

In conclusion, deep learning stands as an epitome of artificial intelligence's evolution—a journey from rudimentary algorithms to intricate neural architectures that comprehend data's intricacies. From image analysis's canvas of pixels to NLP's symphony of words and sequences' temporal melodies, deep learning has altered industries, reshaped economies, and redefined possibilities. As we continue to unearth the depths of deep learning's potential, we step closer to the realization of machines that not only replicate human intelligence but also transcend its limitations, crafting a future where innovation knows no bounds.

Popular deep learning frameworks: TensorFlow and PyTorch

In artificial intelligence and deep learning, the pivotal role of frameworks cannot be overstated. These software platforms provide the scaffolding upon which complex neural networks are built, trained, and deployed, accelerating the pace of innovation in the field. Among the giants that dominate this landscape, TensorFlow and PyTorch stand as titans, offering developers and researchers powerful tools to harness the depths of deep learning. In this section, we embark on a journey to explore the essence of TensorFlow and PyTorch, delving into their histories, functionalities, and how they shape the future of AI.

The ascent of deep learning is intrinsically tied to the development of specialized frameworks that simplify the process of creating and training intricate neural network architectures. Before the inception of such tools, crafting neural networks required meticulous coding of low-level mathematical operations, which hindered the democratization of deep learning. The emergence of frameworks marked a paradigm shift, enabling researchers and practitioners to focus on high-level design and experimentation, while the framework handled the underlying complexities.

TensorFlow, an open-source framework developed by Google Brain, stands as a cornerstone of deep learning innovation. Introduced in 2015, TensorFlow has gained rapid adoption due to its robust capabilities and support for both research and production scenarios. The framework's foundation rests on the concept of tensors— multi-dimensional arrays that represent data. This tensor-centric architecture aligns well with the computations inherent in neural networks and facilitates efficient execution on various hardware, including CPUs, GPUs, and TPUs (Tensor Processing Units).

TensorFlow's strength lies in its versatility. Its high-level APIs offer simplicity for quick prototyping, while its low-level APIs enable fine-grained control and optimization. TensorFlow's ecosystem includes TensorFlow Lite for mobile and embedded devices, TensorFlow Extended (TFX) for machine learning pipelines, and TensorFlow Serving for deploying models at scale. Its integration with tools like TensorBoard for visualization and TensorRT for optimization elevates TensorFlow's status as an end-to-end solution.

PyTorch, developed by Facebook's AI Research lab (FAIR), emerged as an alternative to TensorFlow, offering a dynamic computational graph and a focus on research-oriented exploration. Released in 2016, PyTorch gained traction due to its intuitive interface and the ability to build computational graphs on-the-fly. This dynamic nature enables immediate interaction with tensors, facilitating debugging and experimentation. PyTorch's architecture, centered around tensors and automatic differentiation, aligns with the imperative programming paradigm, making it conducive to dynamic model building.

PyTorch's design ethos resonates with the research community, as it promotes a deep understanding of neural network internals. This feature enables researchers to prototype complex architectures and test hypotheses efficiently. The framework's PyTorch Lightning extension simplifies experiment management, while libraries like torchvision and torchaudio provide tools tailored for image and audio processing tasks. Furthermore, PyTorch's collaboration with popular libraries like NumPy ensures seamless integration into existing workflows.

The choice between TensorFlow and PyTorch hinges on various factors, including the project's goals, user preferences, and the desired level of control. TensorFlow's static computational graph, facilitated by its eager execution mode, is advantageous for optimization and deployment scenarios. However, this architecture can be perceived as less intuitive for experimentation. In contrast, PyTorch's dynamic computation graph is conducive to research and prototyping, enabling easy model building and interactive debugging. PyTorch's dynamic nature, however, can sometimes lead to inefficiencies during execution.

TensorFlow's Keras API, integrated as a high-level interface, simplifies model construction, and its large user base provides a vast repository of pre-trained models and community-contributed resources. PyTorch's native API, while more flexible, demands a steeper learning curve. TensorFlow's robustness and comprehensive ecosystem make it a preferred choice for production environments, especially when scalability and performance are paramount.

Both TensorFlow and PyTorch have left an indelible mark on various industries. In healthcare, these frameworks empower medical image analysis, disease diagnosis, and drug discovery. In finance, they facilitate risk assessment, fraud detection, and algorithmic trading. In autonomous vehicles, they enable perception, decision-making, and sensor fusion. Moreover, these frameworks drive breakthroughs in natural language processing, from language translation to sentiment analysis, and enable the development of sophisticated generative models like GANs.

One of the pivotal factors driving the success of TensorFlow and PyTorch is their open-source nature. These frameworks, freely accessible to researchers, developers, and enterprises, foster collaboration and innovation. The contributions from the global community lead to enhancements, bug fixes, and the creation of novel libraries that expand the frameworks' capabilities. This collaborative ethos accelerates the evolution of deep learning, ensuring that advancements reach a wider audience.

In conclusion, TensorFlow and PyTorch, as pillars of the deep learning landscape, exemplify the synergy between innovation and accessibility. TensorFlow's architectural prowess and comprehensive ecosystem position it as a versatile choice for production scenarios, where efficiency and scalability are paramount. PyTorch, with its dynamic computation graph and research-friendly environment, caters to researchers, enabling them to rapidly experiment, explore, and contribute to the field's advancement.

The tale of TensorFlow and PyTorch is a testament to the power of frameworks—tools that elevate the potential of neural networks and democratize the journey into deep learning. As these frameworks continue to evolve, they paint a canvas of possibilities, where the lines between human and machine intelligence blur, and the enigma of artificial intelligence is gradually unveiled.

CHAPTER IV

Natural Language Processing (NLP)

Introduction to the field of NLP and its importance in today's data-driven world

In the vast landscape of data-driven technologies, a realm that bridges the chasm between human communication and computational analysis has emerged—Natural Language Processing (NLP). As an interdisciplinary field encompassing linguistics, computer science, and artificial intelligence, NLP stands as a testament to humanity's quest to imbue machines with the ability to understand, interpret, and create human language. In this section, we embark on a trip to unravel the intricacies of NLP, its significance, and how it has become the cornerstone of the modern data-driven world.

NLP is rooted in the age-old challenge of enabling computers to comprehend the nuances of human language—a task that often eludes precise rules due to the inherent complexities of grammar, syntax, and semantics. The evolution of NLP mirrors the evolving capabilities of computational systems. Early efforts focused on rule-based systems, which employed predefined linguistic rules to analyze text. However, the inherent ambiguity of language proved formidable, and rule-based approaches struggled to capture the depth and diversity of human expression.

The advent of machine learning and statistical methods marked a pivotal shift in NLP. These approaches allowed computers to learn from large corpora of text, decipher patterns, and make predictions. The transition from rule-based to data-driven methodologies heralded an era of transformation, paving the way for the modern NLP landscape.

NLP encompasses two fundamental aspects—language understanding and language generation. Language understanding involves tasks such as sentiment analysis, named entity recognition, and text classification. These tasks empower machines to comprehend the semantics and intentions embedded in text. For instance, sentiment analysis gauges the emotional tone of text, while named entity recognition identifies entities like names, dates, and locations within text.

On the other side of the spectrum lies language generation, which involves tasks like machine translation, text summarization, and chatbot interaction. These tasks enable machines to generate coherent and contextually relevant text. Machine translation, exemplified by services like Google Translate, enables seamless communication across languages. Text summarization condenses lengthy content while retaining its essence, and chatbots engage in human-like conversations, making them invaluable in customer service and information retrieval.

In today's data-driven world, where information abounds in the form of unstructured text, NLP acts as a catalyst that transforms raw text into actionable insights. Social media platforms generate an ocean of opinions, sentiments, and trends that NLP can analyze to gauge public sentiment and track emerging topics. The financial sector employs NLP to analyze news articles and social media chatter, enhancing investment decisions. In healthcare, NLP extracts valuable information from clinical notes, aiding in diagnoses and treatment planning. Legal professionals leverage NLP for document analysis and contract review, streamlining their operations.

Furthermore, NLP's fusion with other technologies like machine learning, deep learning, and big data analytics amplifies its impact. Deep learning models, particularly Transformer-based architectures, have revolutionized NLP tasks by capturing contextual relationships and generating coherent text. Models like BERT (or Bidirectional Encoder Representations from Transformers) exhibit a deep understanding of language, enabling context-aware language understanding and generation.

While NLP's strides have been remarkable, challenges abound. One of the most formidable obstacles is language's inherent ambiguity. Words can have numerous meanings depending on context, and sentences may be interpreted differently based on cultural and linguistic nuances. The challenge is amplified in languages with complex morphology and syntax. Moreover, the scarcity of labeled data in some languages and domains poses hurdles in training effective models.

Ethical considerations are another dimension of NLP's landscape. Bias, inadvertently introduced by training data, can perpetuate stereotypes and unequal representation. Ensuring that NLP models are fair and unbiased is a critical endeavor. Privacy concerns also arise as NLP models analyze personal and sensitive information, necessitating responsible data handling and governance.

The trajectory of NLP is inexorably intertwined with the evolution of human-machine interaction. The rise of voice assistants including Siri, Alexa, and Google Assistant signifies the growing integration of NLP into daily life. Conversational AI, marked by chatbots and virtual assistants, has the potential to transform customer service, education, and healthcare. These advancements pave the way for natural, intuitive interactions between humans and machines, bridging the gap between technological sophistication and human communication.

In conclusion, natural Language Processing stands as a technological marvel—a convergence of linguistic insights, computational power, and human ingenuity. It has transformed the way we interact with data, unlocking the ability to glean insights from text on a scale never before possible. From language understanding to generation, from sentiment analysis to translation, NLP's impact reverberates across industries, transcending cultural and linguistic barriers.

As NLP continues to evolve, it holds the promise of realizing the dream of seamless communication between humans and machines. It empowers us to explore the depths of language, to understand sentiment, intention, and meaning, and to harness the power of unstructured data in ways that were once beyond imagination. In the modern data-driven world, NLP's importance is not merely technical—it's a bridge that unites human expression with computational analysis, paving the way for a future where language is the conduit through which insights flow, transforming information into wisdom.

Advanced NLP techniques such as sentiment analysis, named entity recognition, and text generation

In Natural Language Processing (NLP), the pursuit of understanding, dissecting, and generating human language has led to the development of advanced techniques that unravel intricate nuances. Among these techniques, sentiment analysis, named entity recognition, and text generation stand as pillars of NLP's evolution. In this section, we embark on a journey into the depths of these advanced NLP techniques, exploring their mechanisms, applications, and the transformative impact they have on industries and communication.

Sentiment analysis, ofeten called opinion mining, is a technique in NLP that involves extracting and quantifying the emotional tone or sentiment expressed within text. This technique empowers machines to discern whether a given piece of text conveys a positive, negative, or neutral sentiment. Sentiment analysis operates on a spectrum, ranging from binary classification (positive/negative) to multi-class classification, capturing nuances like joy, sadness, anger, and surprise.

The applications of sentiment analysis span across industries. In social media monitoring, sentiment analysis gauges public opinions, helping businesses understand customer perceptions and adapt marketing strategies accordingly. In financial markets, sentiment analysis of news articles and social media chatter informs investment decisions. Customer service operations leverage sentiment analysis to prioritize and address customer complaints and feedback promptly. The technique also plays a critical role in political analysis, tracking public sentiment and reactions during elections or policy changes.

Named Entity Recognition (NER) is an NLP technique designed to locate and classify named entities within text, such as names of people, organizations, locations, dates, and more. NER contributes to information extraction by identifying key entities that can be used for indexing, analysis, and retrieval. The technique relies on machine learning models that are trained on annotated datasets to recognize patterns associated with different types of entities.

The importance of NER extends across a myriad of applications. In news articles, NER identifies crucial entities like the names of people, organizations, and locations, aiding in summarization and information retrieval. In healthcare, NER helps extract medical terminologies, patient records, and drug names, facilitating clinical decision-making and research. Legal professionals benefit from NER by streamlining document analysis and contract review, efficiently identifying parties, dates, and legal references.

Text generation, a marvel of NLP, involves training models to create coherent and contextually relevant text. This technique has witnessed revolutionary advancements, particularly with the advent of deep learning models like Transformers. The essence of text generation lies in the model's capacity to learn the inherent structure of language and mimic human-like text production.

One of the most remarkable applications of text generation is language translation. Models like OpenAI's GPT-3 have the ability to translate text from one language to another while preserving context and meaning. Text generation also powers chatbots, virtual assistants, and dialogue systems, enabling human-like interactions across industries. In content creation, automated text generation aids in producing articles, summaries, and even poetry. However, ethical considerations are pivotal, as text generation models must be carefully controlled to avoid generating biased, offensive, or misleading content.

The integration of sentiment analysis, named entity recognition, and text generation has ushered transformative changes across various industries. In media and entertainment, sentiment analysis informs content creation by gauging audience reactions to movies, TV shows, and music. It also helps media outlets understand public sentiment toward news stories and tailor content accordingly. NER assists in content discovery by linking related articles, videos, and resources, enhancing user experience.

In the realm of healthcare, sentiment analysis is employed to monitor patient feedback and assess satisfaction levels. NER aids in clinical research by extracting and categorizing medical terms, patient information, and drug names from electronic health records. Text generation assists doctors in generating patient reports, diagnoses, and treatment plans, streamlining communication and documentation. Financial institutions leverage sentiment analysis to gauge market sentiment and predict stock price movements. NER plays a crucial role in financial news analysis, identifying key entities that influence market trends. Additionally, text generation contributes to the creation of financial reports, investment summaries, and market analyses.

While advanced NLP techniques offer remarkable capabilities, challenges persist. Sentiment analysis accuracy can be influenced by context and sarcasm, demanding nuanced approaches. NER accuracy hinges on the availability of labeled training data and adapting models to domain-specific jargon. Text generation poses ethical concerns, necessitating responsible AI development to mitigate the risk of generating biased, offensive, or harmful content.

The future holds promising horizons for these techniques. Emotion-aware sentiment analysis aims to capture complex emotions beyond binary categorization. NER models are evolving to identify relationships between entities and uncover hidden connections. Text generation models are advancing towards more coherent, contextually aware outputs, enabling even more seamless human-machine communication.
In conclusion, advanced NLP techniques—sentiment analysis, named entity recognition, and text generation—represent milestones in the realm of human-computer interaction. They transform raw text into actionable insights, unveil key entities within data, and enable machines to generate contextually relevant language. The fusion of these techniques permeates industries, informing decision-making, enhancing user experience, and redefining communication.

As NLP techniques continue to evolve, their impact on our lives will be profound. From enhancing customer service interactions to revolutionizing content creation, these techniques enable machines to understand and emulate the complexities of human language. The journey into the world of advanced NLP is a testament to the power of technology to bridge the gap between human expression and computational analysis, forging a future where language is the conduit through which information, insights, and creativity flow.

Pre-trained language models like BERT and GPT for NLP tasks

In the always-changing landscape of Natural Language Processing (NLP), the emergence of pre-trained language models stands as a pivotal moment—a transformation that has redefined the boundaries of linguistic comprehension and paved the way for unprecedented breakthroughs. Among these models, BERT (Bidirectional Encoder Representations from Transformers) and GPT (Generative Pre-trained Transformer) have garnered unparalleled attention for their ability to comprehend, generate, and manipulate human language. In this section, we embark on a trip to unravel the intricacies of pre-trained language models, exploring the mechanics, applications, and the profound impact they have on NLP tasks and beyond.

Language models are at the core of NLP, aiming to impart machines with the ability to understand and generate human language. Early language models were rule-based, relying on handcrafted linguistic rules and structures to process text. However, these models struggled to capture the complexity and variability of human expression, often faltering in the face of ambiguous syntax and context.

The advent of data-driven approaches, particularly those leveraging machine learning and neural networks, ushered a paradigm shift. Instead of relying on rigid rules, these models learned from vast amounts of text data, capturing patterns and relationships that eluded rule-based systems. While these models showcased remarkable improvements, they demanded substantial computational resources and data for training, often limiting their accessibility and usability.

Pre-trained language models, a culmination of data-driven methodologies and transformer architecture, marked a revolutionary leap in NLP. These models embraced the concept of transfer learning—training a model on a massive corpus of text data and then fine-tuning it for specific NLP tasks. This approach leverages the model's pre-existing understanding of language, allowing it to adapt swiftly to new tasks with smaller, task-specific datasets.

BERT, introduced by Google in 2018, shattered conventional language model paradigms by introducing bidirectionality into the learning process. Unlike earlier models that operated in a unidirectional manner, BERT considered both left and right contexts of a word during training. This bidirectional attention mechanism enabled BERT to capture intricate relationships between words, enhancing its understanding of context and meaning. BERT's transformative capabilities span a multitude of NLP tasks. In text classification, it delivers exceptional accuracy by grasping the nuances within sentences. Named Entity Recognition (NER) benefits from BERT's contextual awareness, as it accurately identifies entities within varying linguistic contexts. BERT also excels in question answering, language translation, and even sentiment analysis, where its comprehension of context fosters deeper insights.

Conversely, GPT, pioneered by OpenAI, focuses on the generation of human-like text. It employs a unidirectional approach, predicting the next word in a sequence based on preceding words. This unidirectional training produces coherent text but can lack the bidirectional comprehension that BERT offers. GPT models, however, excel in generating text and have found remarkable applications in content creation, text completion, and even creative writing.

GPT's impact reverberates across industries. In content creation, it assists writers in generating articles, marketing copy, and even scripts. Chatbots and virtual assistants leverage GPT's contextual generation for natural, human-like interactions. Moreover, GPT-3, OpenAI's third iteration, has demonstrated the capacity to write poetry, answer complex questions, and even produce code snippets, showcasing the extent of its creative potential.

Pre-trained language models embody the principles of transfer learning, enabling them to transfer knowledge from one domain to another. Fine-tuning—adapting the model to a specific task with task-specific data—serves as the bridge between the pre-trained model's linguistic understanding and the task's requirements. Fine-tuning is often achieved by training the model on the task-specific data while maintaining the pre-trained weights, thus retaining the underlying language comprehension while refining it for the task at hand.
This approach revolutionizes the NLP landscape, as it mitigates the need for extensive task-specific training data. Instead of training a model from scratch for each task, practitioners can leverage pre-trained models to jumpstart the learning process. This democratizes the use of sophisticated language models and empowers even those with limited data to achieve impressive results.

While pre-trained language models open new vistas, they also raise ethical concerns. Bias, imprinted from the training data, can perpetuate stereotypes and unequal representation. Misinformation generated by these models poses a risk, necessitating careful monitoring and control. Additionally, the environmental impact of training these models, with their enormous computational requirements, is an ongoing concern.

The 'black-box' nature of these models also hinders interpretability. Understanding why a model makes a particular prediction or generates specific text is a challenge, particularly in safety-critical domains like healthcare and law.

The journey of pre-trained language models is an ongoing exploration, with new architectures and enhancements continually reshaping their landscape. BERT's successors, such as RoBERTa, further refine bidirectional understanding. GPT models continue to evolve, exploring new avenues in creative writing, text generation, and even dialogue systems.

Zero-shot and few-shot learning, showcased by GPT-3, hold the promise of training models with minimal task-specific data, expanding the model's adaptability. Multilingual pre-trained models, like mBERT and XLM-R, break language barriers, enabling NLP across diverse linguistic contexts.

In conclusion, pre-trained language models like BERT and GPT epitomize the synergy between linguistic understanding, data-driven learning, and computational might. They have redefined NLP by enabling machines to understand, generate, and manipulate human language with unprecedented accuracy and versatility. From sentiment analysis to text generation, from chatbots to creative writing, these models permeate industries, transform communication, and bridge the gap between human expression and technological ingenuity.

As these models evolve, they will shape the future of NLP, propelling us into an era where language becomes a seamless conduit for communication and insights. The journey of pre-trained language models represents a fusion of linguistics and machine learning—a testament to the human drive to decipher the complexities of language and harness its power to drive innovation and understanding.

CHAPTER V

Computer Vision and Image Processing

Exploration of the role of machine learning in computer vision and image analysis

In the realm of modern technology, the convergence of machine learning and computer vision has birthed a new era of innovation—one that empowers machines to interpret, understand, and derive insights from the visual world. Computer vision, a discipline focused on enabling machines to comprehend images and videos, has been revolutionized by the prowess of machine learning algorithms. In this section, we embark on a journey to explore the profound role of machine learning in computer vision and image analysis, delving into the mechanisms, applications, and transformative impact that this synergy has on industries and human interaction.

Computer vision, at its core, is driven by the human desire to replicate the remarkable ability of our visual system to interpret the world. From deciphering text within images to recognizing faces, objects, and scenes, computer vision aims to equip machines with the power of sight. Early computer vision systems relied on rule-based approaches that outlined explicit instructions for image analysis. However, the complexities of visual data, variations in lighting, and the inherent diversity of scenes made rule-based methods inadequate.

Machine learning, a subset of artificial intelligence, heralded a paradigm shift in the realm of computer vision. Instead of relying on handcrafted rules, machine learning algorithms learn patterns and representations from data. This ability to learn from examples empowers machines to evolve their understanding of images as they encounter more data. The fusion of machine learning with computer vision paved the way for systems capable of image recognition, object detection, segmentation, and even generating content.

Convolutional Neural Networks (CNNs), inspired by the organization of the visual cortex in mammals, emerged as the cornerstone of visual learning. These networks excel in tasks like image classification, object detection, and semantic segmentation. CNNs operate by hierarchically processing image data, progressively extracting features of increasing complexity. The application of convolutional filters allows these networks to capture spatial hierarchies and relationships, enabling them to recognize patterns in images.
CNNs have revolutionized image classification. Models like AlexNet, VGG, ResNet, and Inception have consistently pushed the boundaries of accuracy on benchmarks like ImageNet, showcasing the potential of deep learning in visual tasks. Beyond image classification, CNNs excel in object detection, localizing and classifying objects within images, and semantic segmentation, where every pixel is assigned a class label, contributing to scene understanding.

One of the game-changing aspects of machine learning in computer vision is transfer learning—a concept that empowers models to apply knowledge gained from one task or dataset to another. Transfer learning leverages pre-trained models, often trained on vast datasets, to bootstrap learning on smaller, task-specific datasets. This approach democratizes the power of complex models, enabling even those with limited data to achieve impressive results.

Transfer learning's impact is exemplified by fine-tuning pre-trained CNNs for specific tasks. For instance, models pre-trained on ImageNet, a dataset containing millions of images, can be fine-tuned for tasks like medical image analysis, satellite image interpretation, or even artistic style transfer.

Generative models, another category of machine learning algorithms, have pushed the boundaries of image analysis and creation. These models, including Generative Adversarial Networks (GANs) and Variational Autoencoders (VAEs), produce images that are remarkably similar to real ones. GANs, in particular, consist of a generator and a discriminator that play a cat-and-mouse game, resulting in the generation of images that are increasingly indistinguishable from real ones.

GANs have applications ranging from data augmentation—enhancing training data by generating new samples—to artistic style transfer, where they infuse the style of one image onto the content of another. They also revolutionize tasks like image super-resolution, producing high-quality images from low-resolution inputs, with applications in medical imaging and surveillance. The

fusion of machine learning and computer vision has cast a transformative spell across industries. In healthcare, these technologies enable disease diagnosis through medical image analysis, aiding radiologists in identifying anomalies in X-rays, MRIs, and CT scans. Autonomous vehicles employ computer vision to perceive and navigate the environment, recognizing pedestrians, traffic signs, and obstacles.

Retail industries leverage computer vision for object detection, enabling automated checkout and inventory management. Agriculture benefits from aerial imagery analysis, monitoring crop health and predicting yield. Security and surveillance systems identify suspicious activities and track individuals in crowded environments. While the marriage of machine learning and computer vision holds immense potential, it also poses challenges. Annotating large datasets for training machine learning models demands substantial human effort and expertise. Additionally, models can inherit biases present in training data, perpetuating stereotypes and inequalities. Interpreting and explaining the decisions made by complex deep learning models remains a challenge, particularly in safety-critical applications. As these models process enormous amounts of data, energy consumption and environmental concerns arise, necessitating the development of more efficient architectures.

Machine learning future in computer vision holds promises of enhanced understanding and generative capabilities. Models that understand context and common sense, coupled with those capable of reasoning and decision-making, have the potential to revolutionize visual understanding further.

In conclusion, machine learning's integration with computer vision has kindled a revolution, transforming the visual world from an enigmatic tapestry into a decipherable realm. From deciphering images to generating content, machine learning algorithms like CNNs and GANs have redefined image analysis, fostering insights and creativity that were once beyond imagination.

The symbiosis of machine learning and computer vision transcends industries, from healthcare and transportation to agriculture and entertainment. It encapsulates humanity's aspiration to confer machines with sight and comprehension, transcending the constraints of rule-based systems.

As technology advances and these algorithms continue to evolve, the boundaries of computer vision and image analysis will continually expand, igniting new possibilities and revelations in the visual realm. The exploration of machine learning's role in computer vision is not merely a journey through code and data—it's a voyage into the heart of human perception, transforming our interaction with the visual universe.

Discussion techniques like object detection, image segmentation, and image generation using GANs

In the vast canvas of computer vision, a symphony of techniques orchestrates the interpretation and manipulation of visual data. Among these techniques, object detection, image segmentation, and image generation using Generative Adversarial Networks (GANs) emerge as virtuosic performers—each playing a pivotal role in unveiling the intricate details of images and shaping the future of visual understanding. In this section, we embark on a journey to explore the nuances of these techniques, delving into their mechanics, applications, and the transformative impact they wield on industries, creativity, and the human interaction with the visual world.

Object detection is a cornerstone technique in computer vision, enabling machines to identify and locate objects within images or videos. Unlike image classification, where the focus is on identifying the dominant object in an image, object detection delves deeper, pinpointing the positions of multiple objects and classifying them. This technique is the gateway to understanding the spatial relationships between objects—a fundamental step towards comprehending the visual world.

Early object detection techniques relied on handcrafted features and sliding window approaches. However, the advent of deep learning, particularly Convolutional Neural Networks (CNNs), revolutionized object detection. The region-based CNNs (R-CNN) family, including Faster R-CNN and Mask R-CNN, introduced the concept of proposing regions of interest within an image, optimizing both accuracy and speed.

Applications of object detection span diverse domains. In autonomous vehicles, it empowers vehicles to perceive pedestrians, other vehicles, and obstacles, facilitating safe navigation. In surveillance, it detects unauthorized intrusions and suspicious activities. Retail industries employ it for inventory management and theft prevention. Moreover, medical imaging benefits from object detection by identifying anomalies in X-rays and MRIs, supporting timely diagnosis.

Image segmentation takes the understanding of images a step further by partitioning them into meaningful segments, each representing a distinct object or region. This technique provides granular insights into the composition of images, facilitating more advanced analysis and interpretation. Unlike object detection, image segmentation doesn't just locate objects—it delineates their boundaries with pixel-level precision.

Semantic segmentation, a type of image segmentation, classifies each pixel into specific object categories, effectively labeling every pixel. Fully Convolutional Networks (FCNs) spearheaded the development of semantic segmentation by leveraging CNNs to capture local and global context. Instance segmentation, a more advanced form, distinguishes individual instances of objects, even if they belong to the same category.

Image segmentation permeates various sectors. In medical imaging, it aids in tumor detection and delineation. Agriculture employs it for crop health assessment and disease identification. Autonomous vehicles leverage segmentation to analyze road scenes, demarcating lanes, traffic signs, and pedestrians. Additionally, image editing and content-aware resizing benefit from the precise object boundaries offered by segmentation.

The advent of Generative Adversarial Networks (GANs) marked a paradigm shift in the world of image generation. GANs consist of two networks—the generator and the discriminator—engaged in a cat-and-mouse game. The generator crafts synthetic images, aiming to deceive the discriminator, while the discriminator endeavors to differentiate between real and generated images. Through this adversarial training, GANs generate images that are increasingly indistinguishable from real ones.

Conditional GANs (cGANs) extend this concept, allowing users to influence the generated output by providing conditional information. This paves the way for applications like style transfer and image-to-image translation, where GANs transform images based on user-defined characteristics.

GANs transcend mere replication—they breathe life into imagination. Creative applications range from generating photorealistic artworks to creating virtual characters. Medical imaging benefits from GANs in data augmentation, where they generate variations of medical images, aiding in training robust models. In fashion, GANs inspire designers by generating diverse clothing designs. Moreover, GANs challenge reality with deepfake technology, raising ethical and privacy concerns.

The fusion of these techniques has engendered transformative changes across industries. In agriculture, object detection aids in pest monitoring, ensuring crop health. Retail industries leverage image segmentation for visual search and personalized marketing, analyzing consumer preferences. Autonomous vehicles, powered by object detection and image segmentation, pave the path for safer roads and efficient transportation.

The impact reverberates in creative spheres as well. Art and entertainment industries employ GANs for image synthesis and style transfer, blurring the line between human and machine-generated art. Content creators harness GANs to generate realistic landscapes, characters, and scenes for games and movies.

While these techniques hold immense promise, they encounter challenges. Object detection may falter in crowded or occluded scenarios. Image segmentation faces difficulties with fine-grained boundaries and variations in lighting. GANs, despite their prowess, can produce artifacts and suffer from mode collapse—where they generate a limited variety of outputs.

Ensuring robustness and fairness in these techniques is paramount. Bias in training data can lead to skewed outcomes, perpetuating stereotypes and inequalities. The ethical implications of GANs, particularly deepfakes, call for responsible deployment and awareness.

The future beckons with advancements. Object detection and image segmentation will delve deeper into real-time and multi-modal analysis. GANs will evolve to generate diverse and controllable outputs, playing a more significant role in creative industries and content generation.

In conclusion, object detection, image segmentation, and image generation through GANs constitute the bedrock of modern computer vision, breathing life and comprehension into images. These techniques redefine the way we interact with visual data, enabling machines to interpret, manipulate, and generate imagery with astonishing precision and creativity.

From industries like healthcare, agriculture, and retail to the realms of art and entertainment, these techniques shape our perception of the world and catalyze innovation. As technology advances, the boundaries of these techniques will expand, ushering in a new era of visual exploration and understanding—a testament to the ever-evolving dance between human ingenuity and machine capabilities.

Real-world applications of computer vision in different industries

In the landscape of technology, the marriage of computer vision with human understanding has yielded a symphony of innovations that transcend traditional boundaries. The remarkable capabilities of computer vision algorithms to interpret and analyze visual data have sparked transformative revolutions across industries, reshaping the way we perceive, interact with, and extract value from the visual world. In this section, we embark on a journey to explore the multifaceted applications of computer vision across various industries, uncovering its potential to revolutionize sectors from healthcare and manufacturing to retail and entertainment.

Computer vision's imprint on healthcare has been profound, ushering in a new era of diagnostics, treatment, and patient care. Medical imaging, once confined to two-dimensional interpretations, has evolved into three-dimensional reconstructions and even dynamic visualization. In radiology, computer vision algorithms dissect X-rays, MRIs, and CT scans, identifying anomalies and aiding in early disease detection. Surgical procedures benefit from augmented reality overlays, guiding surgeons with real-time visualizations during intricate operations. Computer vision also empowers telemedicine, enabling remote diagnosis and consultation through video analysis.

Beyond imaging, computer vision monitors patient activities, detecting falls and anomalies in elderly care facilities. It assists in facial recognition for patient identification and access control, streamlining hospital workflows. Additionally, computer vision paves the way for precision medicine, as it analyzes genetic patterns and variations to tailor treatments to individual patients.

Computer vision has revolutionized manufacturing by enhancing production efficiency, quality control, and safety. Automated visual inspections, once labor-intensive, are now seamless through computer vision systems that detect defects, imperfections, and irregularities in real-time. These systems minimize human error and enhance product quality, resulting in cost savings and improved customer satisfaction.

Robotic automation, guided by computer vision, ensures precise assembly and packaging, eliminating the risk of errors. Computer vision-powered robots can navigate unstructured environments, facilitating tasks like material handling, picking, and placing. Moreover, computer vision bolsters predictive maintenance by analyzing visual data from machinery, detecting signs of wear and tear before failures occur, reducing downtime and production halts.

In the realm of retail, computer vision is reshaping customer experiences and optimizing operations. Visual search enables consumers to find products by capturing images, propelling the evolution of e-commerce. Retailers harness computer vision to monitor foot traffic and analyze customer behavior within stores, optimizing store layouts and product placements for better engagement.

Checkout processes are streamlined with cashier-less stores, where computer vision tracks items and automatically charges customers as they leave. Inventory management becomes efficient through computer vision-powered systems that monitor stock levels and identify discrepancies. Augmented reality applications in retail enable customers to virtually try on clothes or visualize furniture placements before making purchase decisions. The automotive industry is at the forefront of computer vision's transformative potential, with applications spanning autonomous vehicles, advanced driver assistance systems, and in-car infotainment. Cameras, LiDAR, and sensors collaborate to provide a comprehensive view of the vehicle's surroundings, enabling autonomous navigation and collision avoidance.

Computer vision algorithms decipher road signs, traffic lights, and lane markings, contributing to safer and more efficient driving. They also analyze driver behavior, alerting drowsy or distracted drivers to maintain attention on the road. Furthermore, computer vision enhances passenger experiences by enabling gesture-based controls, facial recognition for personalized settings, and real-time driver monitoring for safety.

In the realm of entertainment and media, computer vision is revolutionizing the way we consume and interact with content. Augmented reality (or AR) and virtual reality (or VR) experiences immerse users in captivating narratives, transforming storytelling and gaming. Facial recognition technology enhances user engagement by adapting content based on emotional responses and preferences.

Computer vision-powered content recommendation systems analyze user preferences, viewing patterns, and social interactions, curating personalized content suggestions. Additionally, sports broadcasts leverage computer vision to provide real-time analysis, tracking player movements and delivering insightful statistics to enhance viewer experience.

Computer vision is nurturing the agricultural landscape by optimizing crop management, monitoring, and yield prediction. Drones equipped with cameras capture high-resolution images of fields, detecting crop health indicators like disease, nutrient deficiency, and pests. This data informs precise application of fertilizers, pesticides, and irrigation, reducing resource wastage and promoting sustainable practices.
Computer vision's role extends to livestock management, where it monitors animal behavior, health, and feeding patterns, aiding in early disease detection and improved animal welfare. Precision agriculture benefits from computer vision-enabled robotic systems that selectively weed crops, minimizing the use of herbicides.

Security and surveillance have been fundamentally transformed by computer vision, elevating monitoring capabilities and threat detection. Video analytics powered by computer vision track and identify individuals, detect suspicious activities, and trigger alerts in real-time. Facial recognition algorithms aid in access control, authentication, and criminal identification.

Crowd monitoring algorithms assess crowd density and movement patterns, enhancing safety during large events or gatherings. Additionally, computer vision enhances public safety by detecting abandoned objects or unattended baggage in public spaces, mitigating potential threats.

Computer vision plays a role in environmental conservation by monitoring natural resources and ecosystems. Satellite imagery analysis detects deforestation, land degradation, and changes in vegetation patterns, aiding in biodiversity conservation and forest management. Underwater computer vision systems monitor coral reefs, marine life, and pollution levels, contributing to marine conservation efforts. Wildlife conservation benefits from camera traps and drones equipped with computer vision, tracking animal populations and behaviors. The technology assists researchers in studying animal habits and interactions, supporting effective conservation strategies.

While computer vision's potential is immense, it faces challenges. Privacy concerns surround facial recognition and surveillance applications, demanding careful regulation and ethical considerations. The accuracy of computer vision systems across diverse demographic groups is an ongoing challenge, as biased data can lead to skewed outcomes.

The future holds exciting possibilities. Advancements in deep learning architectures, sensor technology, and cloud computing will propel computer vision to new heights. AR and VR experiences will become more immersive, and medical diagnoses more accurate. Autonomous systems will navigate complex environments with greater precision, and industries will harness computer vision for insights and innovation.

In conclusion, computer vision's transformative impact is an ode to human curiosity and innovation. From healthcare to entertainment, manufacturing to agriculture, its applications illuminate possibilities previously confined to imagination. The symphony of algorithms and sensors orchestrates a harmonious convergence, reshaping industries, enriching experiences, and nurturing a future where the visual realm is not only understood but celebrated—an enduring testament to human creativity and technological prowess.

CHAPTER VI

Time Series Analysis and Forecasting

Explanation of the challenges and importance of time series data in various domains

In the intricate fabric of data analysis, time series data emerges as a unique and dynamic thread—an entity that captures the unfolding of events, trends, and phenomena over time. Time series data, characterized by its sequential nature and temporal dependencies, plays a pivotal role in various domains, from finance and healthcare to climate science and industrial operations. However, its intrinsic complexities and contextual significance introduce challenges that demand innovative approaches and a deep understanding of temporal dynamics. In this section, we embark on a journey to explore the challenges and underscore the paramount importance of time series data in diverse domains, shedding light on how it shapes decision-making, predictions, and insights across the spectrum.

Time series data, by its nature, records observations at successive time intervals, presenting a chronological account of evolving phenomena. This temporal sequence can span milliseconds in high-frequency trading, days in weather forecasting, or even years in demographic analysis. This temporal context infuses data with patterns, trends, and seasonality that are otherwise concealed, enabling a nuanced understanding of the phenomena being studied.

Time series data analysis is not devoid of challenges. One of the foremost hurdles is the temporal dependencies that exist within the data. Events at one time point can influence subsequent events, creating intricate relationships that demand sophisticated modeling techniques. Additionally, irregular sampling intervals, missing values, and noisy measurements can impede analysis, rendering traditional approaches ineffective.

Another challenge arises from the dynamic nature of time series data. Patterns and relationships can change over time due to factors like seasonality, trends, and external events. Capturing these changes and adapting models to evolving dynamics require vigilant monitoring and continuous model updating.

Furthermore, the curse of dimensionality can afflict time series data. High-dimensional temporal data, when not managed appropriately, can lead to overfitting and increased computational costs. Balancing the need for detailed information with the risk of complexity becomes a delicate dance.

The importance of time series data reverberates across various domains, driven by its unique ability to unveil temporal dynamics and predict future outcomes. In finance, time series data informs stock market predictions, portfolio management, and risk assessment. Analyzing historical price movements and market trends equips traders and investors with insights to make informed decisions.

In healthcare, time series data from patient monitoring devices capture vital signs, enabling early detection of anomalies and deterioration. Predictive models built on longitudinal patient data aid in prognosis and treatment planning, leading to more efficient and personalized healthcare.

In climate science, time series data from temperature sensors, satellites, and weather stations empower scientists to track climate change patterns, forecast extreme weather events, and understand long-term environmental shifts. These insights guide policies aimed at mitigating climate impacts.

Industrial operations leverage time series data for predictive maintenance, optimizing manufacturing processes, and minimizing downtime. Machines equipped with sensors generate continuous data streams that, when analyzed, indicate signs of wear and impending failures, enabling timely interventions.

Machine learning techniques have emerged as formidable tools in addressing the challenges and extracting insights from time series data. Methods like Autoregressive Integrated Moving Average (ARIMA), Exponential Smoothing, and more advanced algorithms like Long Short-Term Memory (or LSTM) networks and Gated Recurrent Units (or GRUs) excel in capturing temporal dependencies and modeling evolving patterns.

LSTM and GRU networks, variants of Recurrent Neural Networks (RNNs), stand out in handling sequential data like time series. Their ability to remember past observations and adapt to changing contexts makes them suitable for tasks such as stock price prediction, natural language processing, and medical prognosis.

As data generation escalates, particularly in Internet of Things (IoT) applications, the volume and velocity of time series data grow exponentially. Coping with big time series data necessitates scalable algorithms, efficient storage, and real-time processing capabilities. Cloud computing and distributed systems are becoming indispensable tools for managing and analyzing large-scale time series data.

Interdisciplinary collaborations also hold promise. The fusion of domain expertise from various fields—such as machine learning, statistics, and subject-specific knowledge—can yield novel solutions to complex time series challenges.

In conclusion, time series data stands as a testament to the temporal symphony of events that shape our world. Its significance traverses domains, providing invaluable insights that underpin informed decisions, proactive interventions, and predictive models. However, its intricacies, ranging from temporal dependencies to evolving patterns, pose challenges that necessitate innovative methodologies and interdisciplinary collaborations.

As technology advances and data streams continue to swell, the mastery of time series data analysis becomes ever more critical. The convergence of machine learning, scalable computing, and domain expertise promises a future where time series analysis unlocks deeper understanding, enabling us to navigate the intricate tapestry of time with unprecedented clarity and foresight.

Advanced time series techniques like ARIMA, LSTM, and Prophet for forecasting

In the realm of data analysis, the ability to predict future trends and outcomes is a pursuit of paramount importance. Advanced time series techniques have emerged as formidable tools in this endeavor, enabling analysts and data scientists to unravel the mysteries of temporal data and project future patterns. Among these techniques, Autoregressive Integrated Moving Average (ARIMA), Long Short-Term Memory (LSTM) networks, and Prophet stand as pillars of forecasting prowess. In this section, we embark on a journey to explore the intricacies and applications of these advanced time series techniques, shedding light on their mechanics, strengths, and the transformative impact they wield in forecasting diverse phenomena.

Autoregressive Integrated Moving Average (ARIMA) is a cornerstone in time series analysis, embraced for its versatility and applicability across diverse domains. ARIMA combines autoregressive (AR) components that model the relationship between an observation and its past values, moving average (MA) components that capture the reliance between an observation and a residual error, and differencing (I) to achieve stationarity by subtracting consecutive observations.

ARIMA's strength lies in its ability to handle a wide range of time series data, from financial market fluctuations to meteorological trends. It provides a structured framework to understand the underlying patterns and dynamics of data, making it an essential tool for both exploratory analysis and predictive modeling.
Long Short-Term Memory (LSTM) networks, nestled within the realm of deep learning, represent a quantum leap in time series forecasting. LSTMs excel in capturing intricate temporal dependencies, making them adept at modeling complex sequences where earlier values affect later ones. Unlike traditional methods like ARIMA, LSTMs require no assumption of stationarity or linear relationships, rendering them suitable for non-linear and dynamic data patterns.

LSTMs leverage memory cells that can store information over long time intervals, circumventing the vanishing gradient problem that plagues traditional Recurrent Neural Networks (RNNs). This memory mechanism equips LSTMs to capture long-range dependencies, distinguishing them as powerful tools for tasks such as stock price prediction, natural language processing, and medical prognosis.

Prophet, an open-source forecasting tool developed by Facebook, has surged in popularity for its user-friendly approach and remarkable accuracy. Tailored for forecasting time series data with strong seasonal patterns, Prophet combines the strengths of additive regression models and seasonal decomposition. It introduces flexibility by accommodating holidays, special events, and changepoints that can disrupt regular patterns.

Prophet's appeal lies in its intuitive parameters and minimalistic setup. While seasoned data scientists often employ complex models, Prophet caters to users with varying expertise, democratizing the power of forecasting. Its automatic handling of missing data and outliers further streamlines the forecasting process, making it a valuable tool for organizations seeking quick yet reliable insights.

The applications of advanced time series techniques span diverse domains, resonating with the data-driven needs of industries and research fields. In finance, ARIMA, LSTM, and Prophet models forecast stock prices, exchange rates, and commodity prices, facilitating informed investment decisions.

In healthcare, these techniques predict patient outcomes, disease trends, and treatment responses, offering valuable insights for personalized care and medical planning. Meteorological predictions leverage these techniques to forecast weather patterns, aiding disaster preparedness and agricultural planning.

Manufacturing and supply chain management harness ARIMA, LSTM, and Prophet to optimize production schedules, inventory management, and demand forecasting. Retail industries apply these techniques for sales predictions, inventory optimization, and pricing strategies.

Each of these advanced time series techniques carries unique strengths and limitations. ARIMA, while robust and interpretable, assumes linearity and stationary data—a limitation in capturing complex non-linear patterns. LSTM, on the other hand, thrives in capturing intricate dynamics but demands substantial computational resources and expertise to prevent overfitting. Prophet's simplicity can be a double-edged sword—it offers accessible forecasting but may fall short in handling exceptionally irregular or non-seasonal data.

The choice of technique depends on the nature of the data, the desired level of accuracy, and the resources available for modeling and computation. An understanding of the strengths and limitations guides practitioners in selecting the appropriate technique for their specific forecasting task.

As data generation accelerates and technology evolves, the landscape of time series forecasting will continue to transform. Hybrid models that merge the strengths of traditional techniques like ARIMA with the capabilities of deep learning networks like LSTM hold promise. These models strive to capture both short-term fluctuations and long-term trends, presenting a holistic picture of the future.

Interdisciplinary collaborations will also shape the future of time series forecasting. The fusion of domain expertise with advanced modeling techniques can yield predictive models that not only excel in accuracy but also resonate with the contextual intricacies of specific industries.

In conclusion. the world of forecasting thrives at the crossroads of tradition and innovation. Advanced time series techniques like ARIMA, LSTM, and Prophet transcend the limitations of earlier methods, enriching the spectrum of forecasting tools available to analysts, researchers, and decision-makers. These techniques enable us to peer into the temporal horizon, unveiling the trends and patterns that shape our future.
However, no technique is a panacea. The choice of ARIMA, LSTM, or Prophet depends on the unique characteristics of the data, the intricacies of the problem, and the resources available. As data continues to flow and domains evolve, the synergy of human ingenuity and computational power promises a future where forecasting becomes not only a science but an art—a harmonious dance between data, algorithms, and the ever-unfolding tapestry of time.

Examples of time series applications in finance, healthcare, and more

In the grand tapestry of data, time series applications emerge as a compelling narrative—a narrative that unfolds over time, capturing the rhythms and patterns that shape our world. This unique form of data, characterized by its temporal dependencies, serves as a canvas for a multitude of industries to paint predictions, insights, and informed decisions. Finance and healthcare stand as two prime arenas where time series data takes center stage, but its influence extends far beyond, touching realms like climate science, marketing, and industrial operations. In this section, we embark on a journey to explore the applications of time series data in finance, healthcare, and a diverse spectrum of fields, delving into how the power of temporal insights is harnessed to drive innovation and transformation.

The financial domain is a quintessential arena where time series data finds profound resonance. Time series analysis equips financial analysts and traders with the tools to forecast trends, predict asset prices, and navigate the volatile tides of markets. Stock prices, for instance, exhibit intricate temporal dependencies influenced by a multitude of factors, from market sentiment and macroeconomic indicators to geopolitical events. Time series techniques like Autoregressive Integrated Moving Average (ARIMA) and GARCH models provide a robust foundation for stock price predictions. These models capture short-term fluctuations and volatility patterns, aiding in risk assessment and portfolio optimization. Long Short-Term Memory networks, a branch of deep learning, unravel complex non-linear relationships in financial time series, enabling more accurate predictions and algorithmic trading strategies.

Moreover, the financial industry relies on time series data for risk management. Value-at-Risk (VaR) models, often based on historical price movements, estimate potential losses in portfolios, ensuring resilience against adverse market movements. Credit risk assessment leverages time series analysis to gauge repayment probabilities, aiding lenders in making informed credit decisions.

In the realm of healthcare, time series data holds the key to personalization and precision. Patient monitoring devices generate continuous streams of data, ranging from heart rate and blood pressure to glucose levels and EEG readings. Analyzing these time series data streams empowers healthcare providers to detect anomalies, monitor patient health, and make timely interventions.

Time series forecasting finds application in medical prognosis. Longitudinal patient data, when subjected to advanced techniques like LSTM networks, can predict disease progression, treatment responses, and patient outcomes. These forecasts enable personalized treatment plans, optimizing medical interventions based on each patient's unique temporal patterns.

In the context of epidemiology, time series data is indispensable for disease tracking and outbreak prediction. By analyzing historical disease incidence patterns, health organizations can forecast the spread of infectious diseases, allocate resources, and implement timely public health interventions.

Climate science relies heavily on time series data to decipher the complex dynamics of our planet's ecosystems. Temperature records, ocean currents, atmospheric pressure, and greenhouse gas concentrations constitute time series data that reveal the trends and shifts shaping our climate.

Time series analysis aids climate scientists in understanding long-term climate trends, identifying patterns of global warming, and predicting extreme weather events. Models built on time series data project future climate scenarios, guiding policymakers and societies in mitigating climate change impacts.

In the world of marketing, time series data illuminates consumer behavior, facilitating targeted campaigns and personalized experiences. Transaction histories, website clicks, and social media interactions generate time-stamped data that captures the evolution of customer preferences and engagement.

Time series analysis in marketing includes customer segmentation based on historical purchase behavior, allowing businesses to tailor product recommendations and marketing strategies. Time series forecasting models predict demand fluctuations, optimizing inventory management and supply chain operations.
Industrial operations, from manufacturing to energy production, benefit from time series data analysis. Sensors embedded in machinery generate continuous data streams that reveal operational dynamics, maintenance requirements, and production patterns.

Predictive maintenance leverages time series techniques to identify signs of machinery deterioration, preventing unplanned downtime and costly repairs. Energy consumption patterns, captured through time series data, aid in load forecasting, optimizing resource allocation, and enhancing energy efficiency.
Time series data plays a crucial role in transportation systems, from traffic management to route optimization. Traffic flow data, collected through sensors and cameras, enables real-time traffic monitoring, congestion prediction, and adaptive signal control.

Public transportation systems use time series data to determine optimal schedules and routes, enhancing efficiency and passenger satisfaction. Additionally, time series analysis contributes to the development of autonomous vehicles, as historical sensor data informs decision-making algorithms that navigate complex environments.

While the applications of time series data are myriad, challenges persist. Data quality issues, such as missing values and noise, can hinder accurate analysis. Temporal dependencies, which are inherent in time series data, demand advanced modeling techniques that capture complex relationships.

Domain-specific intricacies also pose challenges. In finance, for instance, the non-stationarity and sudden shifts of financial data demand adaptive models that evolve with market conditions. In healthcare, individual patient variations introduce complexities in disease forecasting and treatment planning.

Interdisciplinary collaborations hold the promise of addressing these challenges. The fusion of domain expertise, data science, and advanced modeling techniques can yield more accurate and contextually relevant insights.

In conclusion, time series data unfurls as a thread that binds diverse industries, illuminating trends, enabling predictions, and shaping informed decisions. From finance and healthcare to climate science and marketing, the applications of time series data are as varied as the fields they influence. As technology advances and data generation accelerates, the significance of time series analysis continues to burgeon.

Through the lens of time, we gain the power to perceive patterns, anticipate shifts, and navigate uncertainty. The applications of time series data underscore the symbiotic relationship between data and human understanding—a relationship that propels innovation, drives progress, and empowers us to decode the enigmatic language of time.

CHAPTER VII

Unsupervised Learning and Clustering

Introduction to the concept of unsupervised learning and its applications

In the realm of machine learning, the journey often begins with labeled data—a trove of examples that guide algorithms toward recognizing patterns and making predictions. However, the real world is brimming with unstructured, unlabeled data that defies easy categorization. Enter unsupervised learning—a paradigm that unlocks the latent potential of this uncharted territory. Unsupervised learning, an essential branch of machine learning, is imbued with the power to unearth hidden structures, groupings, and relationships within data without the crutch of predefined labels. In this section, we embark on a journey to demystify the concept of unsupervised learning, unveiling its principles, methodologies, and a tapestry of applications that span from clustering and dimensionality reduction to anomaly detection and recommendation systems.

Unsupervised learning unfurls as a realm of exploration where algorithms autonomously decipher the inherent structures of data without the guidance of labeled outcomes. Unlike supervised learning, where algorithms are guided by ground truth labels, unsupervised learning steps into the realm of the unknown, driven by the insatiable curiosity to unravel patterns, connections, and groupings that lie beneath the surface.

Two prominent unsupervised learning techniques are clustering and dimensionality reduction. Clustering algorithms unearth natural groupings within data, separating it into distinct clusters where instances share similarities. Dimensionality reduction, on the other hand, pares down the complexity of data by projecting it into a lower-dimensional space while preserving its essential characteristics.

Clustering, a cornerstone of unsupervised learning, is akin to finding hidden constellations in a starlit sky. Algorithms like K-Means and Hierarchical Clustering illuminate inherent groupings within data points, facilitating understanding, segmentation, and decision-making. Applications span a broad spectrum—from customer segmentation in marketing to species classification in biology.

In marketing, clustering identifies segments of customers with similar preferences, allowing tailored marketing strategies. In biology, it classifies DNA sequences into distinct groups, aiding evolutionary analysis. Moreover, clustering nurtures anomaly detection, where deviations from established clusters signal potential fraud, faults, or outliers.

Dimensionality reduction stands as a compass guiding us through the labyrinth of high-dimensional data. The curse of dimensionality plagues many data-driven endeavors, introducing computational burdens and risking overfitting. Techniques like Principal Component Analysis (or PCA) and t-Distributed Stochastic Neighbor Embedding (or t-SNE) distill the essence of data by projecting it onto a lower-dimensional subspace, preserving its most informative components.

In image processing, dimensionality reduction accelerates feature extraction by condensing pixel data while retaining salient visual cues. In genomics, it simplifies genetic data analysis by reducing the number of features without sacrificing meaningful patterns. Dimensionality reduction also kindles interpretability, rendering complex models understandable to human insights.

Anomaly detection serves as a sentinel guarding against the unexpected in data. Unsupervised techniques cast a discerning eye on the data landscape, flagging instances that deviate from established norms. In cybersecurity, anomaly detection detects unauthorized activities by identifying abnormal patterns of network traffic. In industrial operations, it identifies machinery malfunctions by contrasting real-time sensor readings with historical patterns.

Unsupervised anomaly detection evolves alongside the data it monitors. By learning normal behavior over time, it adapts to changes, rendering it applicable across dynamic domains where anomalies might shift in nature and intensity.

Recommendation systems epitomize the marriage of unsupervised learning and user-centric intelligence. These systems navigate vast datasets to offer users personalized suggestions—be it movies, products, or content. Collaborative filtering, a prominent technique, groups users based on their preferences and aligns them with like-minded peers to infer preferences.

E-commerce platforms harness recommendation systems to enhance user engagement and sales. Streaming services employ them to curate playlists and recommend shows. Their potency lies in their ability to unearth latent preferences, foster discovery, and amplify user satisfaction.

The applications of unsupervised learning are as diverse as the landscapes they encompass. In finance, unsupervised learning identifies market segments, detects anomalies in financial transactions, and refines portfolio optimization. In healthcare, it aids in patient segmentation, unsupervised disease discovery, and analysis of gene expression patterns.

Natural language processing leverages unsupervised learning to mine text data, uncover latent topics, and classify documents. In autonomous vehicles, it clusters sensor data to distinguish between road elements and identify potential obstacles.

Unsupervised learning is not devoid of challenges. The absence of labeled data introduces ambiguity, demanding rigorous evaluation metrics. Interpretability remains a concern, as unsupervised models might unveil patterns without providing the context behind them.

The future holds exciting prospects. Hybrid models that blend supervised and unsupervised techniques can leverage the strengths of both paradigms. As data streams amplify and unstructured data proliferates, unsupervised learning will evolve to unveil the complexities of the data deluge, pioneering innovative solutions and reshaping industries.

In conclusion, unsupervised learning transcends the boundaries of labeled data, unfurling a realm of exploration and discovery. From the art of clustering and the science of dimensionality reduction to the vigilance of anomaly detection and the intuition of recommendation systems, unsupervised learning weaves patterns, reveals insights, and guides decisions. Its applications span a multitude of industries, enhancing efficiency, personalization, and understanding.

As technology advances and data accumulates, unsupervised learning stands poised to unlock new dimensions of knowledge. It unveils the latent beauty of the unexplored, showcasing the power of algorithms to decipher, interpret, and appreciate the intricate tapestry woven by the world of data.

Various clustering techniques like k-means, hierarchical clustering, and DBSCAN

In the vast landscape of data analysis, the art of uncovering hidden structures and groupings within datasets stands as a cornerstone of understanding. Clustering, a fundamental technique in unsupervised learning, emerges as a powerful tool to fulfill this endeavor. At the heart of clustering lies the quest to partition data points into meaningful clusters, where instances within each cluster exhibit similarities while differing from instances in other clusters. Among the multitude of clustering techniques, K-Means, Hierarchical Clustering, and DBSCAN (or Density-Based Spatial Clustering of Applications with Noise) stand as beacons of clustering prowess. In this section, we embark on a journey to explore these clustering techniques, delving into their mechanisms, strengths, and diverse applications that span from customer segmentation to anomaly detection.

K-Means, a celebrated algorithm, casts a spotlight on data point centrality. It orchestrates a symphony where data points dance to the rhythm of cluster centroids. The algorithm starts by randomly placing centroids in the data space and assigning each data point to the nearest centroid. Centroids then recalibrate to the mean of the data points within their cluster. This interplay between assignments and centroid adjustments continues iteratively until convergence, when data points settle into clusters.

K-Means is characterized by its simplicity and efficiency, making it a favored choice for applications where cluster shapes are relatively spherical and evenly distributed. Customer segmentation in marketing exemplifies one such application. K-Means segregates customers into groups with similar buying behaviors, enabling targeted marketing strategies and personalized experiences. However, K-Means struggles with non-linear cluster shapes and outliers, as it seeks to minimize distances between data points and centroids.
Hierarchical Clustering beckons us to the realm of dendrograms—a visualization that captures the essence of cluster relationships. The algorithm unrolls like a narrative where each data point starts as a singleton cluster and gradually assembles into larger clusters. Agglomerative Hierarchical Clustering begins by merging the closest data points into a cluster and iteratively conglomerating until all data points unite into a single cluster. Divisive Hierarchical Clustering, conversely, begins with all data points in a single cluster and gradually splits them into smaller clusters.

The power of hierarchical clustering lies in its capacity to capture the global and local structures in data. It gracefully accommodates clusters of varying shapes and sizes, making it valuable for applications where data exhibit hierarchical relationships. In biology, hierarchical clustering deciphers gene expression patterns, unveiling genetic relationships and evolutionary pathways.

However, hierarchical clustering's complexity can become a computational burden for large datasets, and its sensitivity to outliers demands preprocessing and careful interpretation.

Density-Based Spatial Clustering of Applications with Noise sets a different tone in the clustering symphony. It navigates data points based on density and builds clusters around dense regions while considering less dense areas as noise. The algorithm starts by selecting a data point and exploring its neighborhood within a specified radius. If the neighborhood contains sufficient data points, a cluster forms. The exploration continues iteratively until all data points are classified into clusters or noise.

DBSCAN's appeal lies in its adaptability to various cluster shapes and sizes, its ability to detect outliers, and its robustness to noise. It thrives in applications where clusters have irregular shapes or exhibit varying densities. Anomaly detection in industrial operations exemplifies DBSCAN's application. It identifies machinery malfunctions by isolating data points that do not conform to dense clusters, signifying potential faults or anomalies. The applications of clustering techniques extend beyond customer segmentation and anomaly detection. In genetics, clustering reveals genetic variations and evolutionary relationships. In image processing, it aids in image segmentation by grouping pixels with similar attributes. Social network analysis employs clustering to detect communities within networks, guiding understanding of social dynamics. Environmental science employs clustering to classify species based on shared characteristics.
In crime analysis, clustering identifies crime hotspots by grouping locations with similar crime patterns. Marketing

harnesses clustering to segment markets, tailor advertising, and optimize product recommendations. Sentiment analysis uses clustering to group similar opinions, facilitating accurate sentiment interpretation.

K-Means, Hierarchical Clustering, and DBSCAN each possess strengths and limitations that guide their choice based on data characteristics and application requirements. K-Means excels in simplicity and efficiency, but it struggles with non-spherical clusters and sensitivity to initializations. Hierarchical Clustering embraces hierarchical structures but can be computationally intensive and sensitive to noise. DBSCAN robustly captures clusters of varying shapes and detects outliers, yet its performance can degrade with varying densities and dimensions.

The choice of clustering technique requires careful consideration of data distribution, cluster shapes, dataset size, and the presence of noise. Hybrid approaches that merge the strengths of multiple techniques aim to harness the best of both worlds, overcoming individual limitations and fostering more accurate cluster discovery. As data generation escalates and technology advances, the realm of clustering evolves. Emerging techniques seek to address the limitations of traditional methods, enhancing their adaptability to complex data landscapes. Hybrid models that combine clustering with other machine learning paradigms like deep learning and reinforcement learning stand as exciting prospects.

Interdisciplinary collaborations between domain experts and data scientists will shape the future of clustering. Domain-specific insights will guide the development of clustering techniques that resonate with the contextual nuances of various industries.

In conclusion, the world of clustering techniques epitomizes the art of discovering order amidst chaos—a symphony that uncovers hidden structures within data. K-Means, Hierarchical Clustering, and DBSCAN represent distinct notes in this symphony, each resonating with unique strengths and capabilities. Their applications span a diverse array of industries, illuminating patterns in genetics, segregating customers in marketing, and guarding against anomalies in industrial operations.

The evolution of clustering techniques mirrors the evolution of data analysis itself—a journey that dances between innovation and tradition, guided by the pursuit of understanding the intricate rhythms and melodies that form the tapestry of our data-driven world.

Use cases in customer segmentation, anomaly detection, and more

In the modern data-driven landscape, the tapestry of information weaves a complex narrative of possibilities. From business decisions to risk assessment, the power of data lies in its potential to uncover patterns, predict trends, and guide informed choices. Among the myriad applications, two prominent domains shine brightly: customer segmentation and anomaly detection. However, the reach of data's influence extends beyond these realms, touching recommendation systems, fraud detection, and beyond. In this section, we delve into these diverse use cases, exploring how data-driven techniques illuminate insights, foster efficiency, and drive innovation in today's interconnected world.

Customer segmentation stands as a beacon of personalization in a sea of products and services. In a world flooded with options, understanding customer preferences, behaviors, and needs is paramount. Segmentation techniques group customers based on shared characteristics, enabling tailored marketing strategies, targeted advertising, and enhanced customer experiences.

Imagine a retail giant seeking to optimize its marketing efforts. By segmenting customers into groups with similar buying behaviors and preferences, the retailer can tailor promotions, advertisements, and product recommendations to resonate with each group's unique interests. The power of customer segmentation lies in its ability to transform data into actionable insights, guiding organizations toward strategies that speak directly to their audience.

Anomaly detection emerges as a sentinel in the realm of data analysis—a guardian against the unexpected, the unusual, and the aberrant. This technique, driven by the quest to identify outliers and deviations from established norms, finds applications in diverse fields ranging from finance to industrial operations.

Consider a financial institution monitoring transactions for signs of fraud. Anomaly detection algorithms scrutinize transaction records, flagging instances that deviate from established spending patterns. By promptly identifying unusual activities, these algorithms save financial institutions from losses and protect customers from unauthorized access.

In the realm of manufacturing, anomaly detection safeguards industrial processes. Sensors embedded in machinery capture real-time data, and anomaly detection algorithms analyze this data to detect deviations from standard performance. Sudden temperature spikes, unusual vibrations, or unexpected fluctuations in pressure can signal impending machinery failures. By detecting anomalies early, manufacturers can schedule maintenance before equipment breakdowns disrupt production.

The digital age has ushered in an era of information overload, where choices are abundant but time is scarce. Recommendation systems emerge as beacons of guidance, offering users tailored suggestions that align with their preferences. These systems leverage data-driven insights to anticipate user needs, fostering engagement, and enhancing user satisfaction.

Streaming platforms exemplify the prowess of recommendation systems. By analyzing user behavior—such as viewing history and genre preferences—these systems curate personalized playlists and movie recommendations. The data-driven intimacy of these suggestions bolsters user retention and paves the path to discovery.

E-commerce platforms also harness the power of recommendation systems to guide purchasing decisions. By analyzing browsing history, purchase patterns, and even demographics, these systems offer personalized product recommendations. The result is an enhanced shopping experience that encourages users to explore a wider range of offerings and make informed choices.

In the digital economy, financial transactions span continents and currencies, necessitating vigilant fraud detection mechanisms. These mechanisms deploy data analytics to detect suspicious patterns, thwarting unauthorized access and protecting users' assets. Consider

the world of credit card transactions. Fraud detection algorithms analyze transaction histories, scrutinizing for patterns that deviate from the norm. For instance, if a card is suddenly used for high-value international purchases after a history of local transactions, the algorithm may flag the activity as potential fraud. This data-driven vigilance safeguards users and financial institutions alike.

Beyond the realm of finance, healthcare also relies on fraud detection techniques to combat insurance fraud. By analyzing claims data, these techniques identify patterns of behavior that deviate from established norms. Frequent claims, unusual billing patterns, or duplicate claims for the same treatment can signal fraudulent activities. Detecting and preventing such behavior not only saves resources but also ensures that legitimate claims are processed efficiently.

In the realm of healthcare, data-driven techniques are revolutionizing treatment strategies. Patient data, ranging from medical history to genetic information, serves as the bedrock for personalized medicine—an approach that tailors treatments to individual patients' unique characteristics.

Consider oncology, where patient data guides treatment decisions. Analyzing genetic profiles and disease history, data-driven models identify treatments most likely to be effective for a specific patient's cancer type. This precision minimizes unnecessary side effects and maximizes treatment efficacy, propelling patient-centric care.

In addition to treatment decisions, healthcare providers also leverage data-driven techniques for disease diagnosis. Machine learning algorithms trained on medical images, such as X-rays and MRIs, can accurately identify anomalies that might be missed by human observers. The ability to identify early signs of diseases like cancer can significantly improve patient outcomes and survival rates.

In the world of supply chain management, data-driven techniques optimize operations, streamline logistics, and enhance efficiency. These techniques harness historical data, real-time monitoring, and predictive analytics to anticipate demand, allocate resources, and navigate supply chain complexities.

Imagine a global retail chain managing inventory across numerous locations. By analyzing historical seasonal trends, sales data, and geographic preferences, data-driven models forecast demand fluctuations. Armed with these predictions, the chain optimizes inventory levels, minimizing overstock and stockouts while maximizing profits.

Data-driven supply chain optimization extends beyond retail. In the agricultural sector, data analytics help optimize planting and harvesting schedules based on weather patterns, soil conditions, and market demand. This ensures that resources are used efficiently, minimizing waste and enhancing overall productivity. The urgency of climate change has propelled energy management to the forefront of global priorities. Data-driven techniques play a pivotal role in optimizing energy consumption, reducing waste, and fostering sustainability.

Smart grids exemplify this role. By analyzing real-time data on energy consumption, generation, and distribution, smart grids adjust operations in response to demand fluctuations. These adjustments optimize energy distribution, reduce transmission losses, and minimize the need for excess energy production, ultimately contributing to a more sustainable energy landscape.

Beyond smart grids, data-driven energy management extends to buildings and homes. Internet of Things (IoT) devices collect data on energy usage, temperature fluctuations, and occupancy patterns. Data analytics identify opportunities for energy savings, such as adjusting thermostat settings during periods of low occupancy or optimizing lighting schedules. These small adjustments, driven by data insights, collectively contribute to a significant reduction in consumption of energy.

In a world abuzz with data, the applications of data-driven techniques are boundless. From enhancing customer experiences and guarding against anomalies to revolutionizing healthcare and advancing sustainability, data's influence radiates across industries and domains.

The common thread in these applications is the quest for insight—the desire to transform data into understanding, complexity into clarity, and uncertainty into informed choices. As technology evolves, data-driven techniques will continue to shape industries, driving innovation, fostering efficiency, and propelling humanity toward a future where insights illuminate possibilities and data remains the catalyst for transformation.

CHAPTER VIII

Reinforcement Learning

An explanation of the fundamentals of reinforcement learning and its connection to real-world decision-making

In artificial intelligence and machine learning, one paradigm stands out for its remarkable ability to simulate and improve decision-making processes—reinforcement learning. Rooted in the principles of behavioral psychology, reinforcement learning has evolved into a powerful framework that mirrors the way humans learn through trial and error. From training autonomous agents to play games to optimizing supply chains and robotics, reinforcement learning bridges the gap between algorithms and real-world decision-making. In this section, we embark on a journey to unravel the fundamentals of reinforcement learning, delving into its core concepts, algorithms, and its intricate connection to real-world scenarios where choices matter.

At the heart of reinforcement learning lies the concept of learning by interacting with an environment. Much like a child navigating the world, a reinforcement learning agent learns through a trial and error, adjusting its actions based on the outcomes it receives. This process is governed by the interplay of three key components: the agent, the environment, and the reward signal.

The agent, often an algorithm or a software agent, takes actions within an environment. The environment is the condition in which the agent operates—be it a virtual world, a physical space, or a simulated scenario. The reward signal serves as the feedback mechanism, quantifying the goodness or badness of an agent's action. By navigating the environment, taking actions, and receiving rewards, the agent gradually hones its decision-making strategy to maximize cumulative rewards over time.

A fundamental challenge in reinforcement learning is the exploration-exploitation trade-off. As the agent seeks to maximize its rewards, it must strike a balance between exploring new actions to discover potentially better strategies and exploiting known actions to reap immediate rewards. Straying too far into exploration might delay optimal decision-making, while overexploitation might lead to missed opportunities. Consider an algorithm learning to play a game. Initially, it explores various moves to understand the game dynamics. As it gathers experience, it starts to exploit actions that have historically yielded higher rewards. Balancing exploration and exploitation is a nuanced dance, often guided by strategies like epsilon-greedy policies or Thompson sampling, where the agent leverages uncertainty to make exploratory choices.

To formalize the reinforcement learning framework, Markov Decision Processes (or MDPs) offer a mathematical framework for modeling decision-making in uncertain environments. MDPs consist of states, actions, transition probabilities, rewards, and discount factors. States represent the current situation, actions denote the available choices, transition probabilities capture the likelihood of moving from one state to another due to an action, and rewards quantify the immediate consequences of actions. The discount factor balances the agent's preference for immediate rewards with long-term cumulative rewards.

MDPs offer a structured representation of decision-making, enabling reinforcement learning algorithms to navigate complex scenarios. This formalism serves as a bridge between the real-world dynamics and the agent's learning process, facilitating the translation of real-world challenges into algorithms that optimize decisions.

Reinforcement learning encompasses a spectrum of algorithms, each designed to address specific challenges and scenarios. Q-Learning is a prominent algorithm in this landscape, centered around estimating the value of state-action pairs. The Q-value represents the expected cumulative reward an agent can obtain by starting from a specific state, taking a particular action, and following a given policy thereafter. Q-Learning iteratively updates Q-values based on the observed rewards and the agent's exploratory actions, converging toward an optimal Q-value function that guides decision-making.

Policy Gradient methods, on the other hand, focus on directly optimizing the agent's policy—a strategy that maps states to actions. By evaluating the performance of the policy using techniques like Monte Carlo methods or value function approximations, these algorithms adjust the policy's parameters to enhance decision-making performance.

Reinforcement learning's prowess extends beyond algorithms—it bridges the gap between computational processes and real-world decision-making scenarios. This connection is illuminated across a plethora of domains where decisions influence outcomes. Autonomous driving serves as an illustrative example. Self-driving cars navigate complex environments, making real-time decisions to ensure safety and efficiency. Reinforcement learning equips these vehicles with the ability to learn from interactions with real-world traffic, weather conditions, and pedestrian behaviors.

Supply chain optimization also showcases reinforcement learning's real-world connection. In the intricate world of logistics, decisions such as inventory management, route planning, and demand forecasting influence operational efficiency. Reinforcement learning algorithms navigate this complexity, factoring in uncertainties and dynamically adapting strategies to maximize profit, minimize costs, and ensure timely deliveries. Reinforcement learning, while powerful, presents challenges that reflect the intricacies of real-world decision-making. The exploration-exploitation trade-off demands sophisticated strategies that balance learning with efficient decision-making. Sparse rewards, where the agent receives feedback infrequently, can hinder learning. Furthermore, the transfer of learned policies to new environments remains a challenge, as small variations in conditions might require significant adaptation.

The future of reinforcement learning holds exciting prospects. Hybrid approaches that blend reinforcement learning with other techniques, such as imitation learning or meta-learning, aim to enhance learning efficiency and transferability. Developments in deep reinforcement learning, where neural networks process complex data inputs, enable the modeling of high-dimensional real-world scenarios.

In the evolving landscape of artificial intelligence and machine learning, reinforcement learning shines as a beacon of decision-making empowerment. Rooted in psychology's principles and powered by algorithmic sophistication, reinforcement learning mirrors the human capacity to learn from experience and optimize actions. From training game-playing agents to enhancing supply chain efficiency and autonomous systems, the journey from algorithms to real-world choices finds its bridge in reinforcement learning. As technology advances and challenges are met, reinforcement learning will continue to amplify human potential by enabling smarter, more adaptive, and more effective decision-making across diverse domains.

Discussion of algorithms like Q-learning, policy gradients, and deep reinforcement learning

In the grand tapestry of artificial intelligence, few threads are as intriguing and impactful as reinforcement learning —a paradigm that empowers machines to learn through interactions and optimize decisions. Among the constellation of algorithms that illuminate this landscape, Q-Learning, Policy Gradients, and Deep Reinforcement Learning stand as beacons of innovation. These algorithms encapsulate diverse strategies for navigating complex decision spaces, from training game-playing agents to optimizing industrial processes and robotics. In this section, we delve into the heart of these algorithms, exploring their mechanics, strengths, and real-world applications that illuminate their transformative potential in the realm of artificial intelligence.

At the cornerstone of reinforcement learning lies Q-Learning—a timeless algorithm that unfurls the realm of value-based decision-making. Q-Learning revolves around the concept of Q-values, which represent the expected cumulative reward an agent can accrue by taking a specific action from a particular state and following an optimal policy thereafter. The algorithm iteratively refines Q-values as the agent explores the environment and receives rewards, gradually converging towards the optimal Q-value function.

The elegance of Q-Learning is its ability to navigate complex state-action spaces, from simple grid worlds to intricate video game environments. Consider the realm of video games where agents, armed with Q-Learning, master the art of playing—training in virtual worlds to achieve superhuman performance. The iconic example is DeepMind's AlphaGo, which utilized Q-Learning variants to dominate the ancient game of Go, a testament to Q-Learning's adaptability and potency.

Policy Gradients illuminate a different facet of reinforcement learning—the art of optimizing policies that map states to actions directly. Rather than estimating Q-values, policy gradient algorithms focus on enhancing the agent's decision-making strategy itself. These algorithms leverage gradient ascent techniques to iteratively adjust the policy's parameters, steering the agent towards actions that maximize rewards.

The power of policy gradients shines in scenarios where action spaces are continuous and high-dimensional. For instance, robotics tasks require a seamless blend of motions to accomplish complex objectives. Policy gradient algorithms guide robotic arms to learn tasks such as object manipulation or assembly by iteratively refining policies. The connection to real-world applications is palpable, as robots equipped with learned policies tackle tasks in manufacturing, healthcare, and even space exploration.

As technology marches forward, the integration of deep learning with reinforcement learning becomes a transformative force—ushering in the era of Deep Reinforcement Learning (DRL). Deep neural networks, with their capacity to process complex data inputs, synergize with reinforcement learning paradigms to tackle high-dimensional problems that were previously out of reach. DRL marries perception with decision-making, enabling agents to learn from raw sensory inputs and perform intricate tasks.

The fusion of DRL with robotics illustrates this synergy. Robots endowed with sensors gather visual or sensory information from their environment. DRL algorithms process this data, mapping perceptions to actions that navigate tasks in unstructured environments. Autonomous vehicles, for instance, leverage DRL to navigate urban landscapes, interpreting camera inputs to make driving decisions that consider traffic, pedestrians, and road conditions.

A common thread across these algorithms is the enigma of exploration and exploitation—an elemental challenge in reinforcement learning. As agents strive to maximize cumulative rewards, they must grapple with the dilemma of choosing known actions that yield immediate benefits (exploitation) versus exploring new actions to unearth potential improvements (exploration). Balancing is essential for effective learning.

Q-Learning addresses this challenge through epsilon-greedy strategies—combining exploitation with occasional exploratory actions. Policy gradient algorithms tackle it by adjusting the balance as learning progresses. Deep

Reinforcement Learning often employs techniques like ε-greedy policies or Boltzmann exploration, leveraging uncertainty to guide exploration.

The applications of these algorithms span a spectrum of domains—showcasing their prowess in diverse scenarios. Q-Learning, with its emphasis on Q-values, finds its home in training agents for game-playing scenarios. Beyond AlphaGo, it powers game agents that master Atari games or navigate complex virtual worlds.

Policy gradient algorithms shine in fields like robotics and industrial optimization. They empower machines to learn delicate and precise actions—opening doors to agile robots that perform surgeries, drones that navigate disaster zones, and automated systems that optimize manufacturing processes.

Deep Reinforcement Learning's impact radiates across domains. In autonomous driving, it underpins self-driving vehicles that learn from real-world data to navigate roads. Healthcare benefits as robots equipped with DRL assist in surgeries, drug discovery, and even elder care. Finance embraces DRL to optimize trading strategies in complex markets.

While these algorithms hold transformative potential, they also confront challenges reflective of their complexity. The exploration-exploitation trade-off is a recurring puzzle, requiring strategies that balance learning and optimal decision-making. Sparse rewards— where feedback is infrequent—can hinder convergence, necessitating techniques that encourage learning.

The horizon ahead is a blend of challenges and opportunities. Hybrid approaches that amalgamate Q-Learning and policy gradients seek to harness the strengths of both worlds. Explorations into safe reinforcement learning aim to mitigate the risks associated with trial and error learning, enabling safer interactions with real-world environments.

In conclusion, Q-Learning, Policy Gradients, and Deep Reinforcement Learning collectively form the vanguard of artificial intelligence's journey into decision-making mastery. These algorithms illuminate the intersection of algorithms and reality, guiding agents from games to industries, from learning to optimize game strategies to orchestrating intricate robotic tasks. As technology advances, challenges are met, and new paradigms emerge, these algorithms will continue to shape the landscape of AI, propelling us towards a future where machines learn, adapt, and optimize decisions with unparalleled finesse.

Applications of reinforcement learning in robotics, gaming, and autonomous systems

In the grand tapestry of technological evolution, few threads are as captivating and transformative as reinforcement learning—a paradigm that endows machines with the ability to learn and optimize decisions through interactions. Within this paradigm, the applications of reinforcement learning are vast and diverse, extending across domains that include robotics, gaming, and autonomous systems. Each of these realms showcases the profound impact of reinforcement learning algorithms, from imbuing robots with agility and adaptability to crafting immersive gaming experiences and paving the way for self-driving vehicles. This section delves into the fabric of these applications, exploring how reinforcement learning reshapes these domains, redefines possibilities, and catalyzes innovation.

Robotics, with its fusion of mechanics and intelligence, emerges as a prime canvas for the application of reinforcement learning. In this context, reinforcement learning propels robots beyond programmed routines, enabling them to adapt, learn from experience, and optimize actions in response to dynamic environments. This adaptability is crucial as robots transition from controlled settings to real-world scenarios with inherent uncertainties.

Consider the world of industrial automation, where robots navigate intricate tasks like pick-and-place operations or assembly. Reinforcement learning equips these robots to refine their actions over time, adapting to variations in object positions, environmental conditions, and unforeseen obstacles. This adaptability enhances manufacturing efficiency, accelerates production, and minimizes downtime.

Robotic manipulation exemplifies the fusion of reinforcement learning's power with real-world applications. Robots with dexterous limbs learn to grasp objects of varying shapes and sizes through trial and error. Reinforcement learning algorithms guide the exploration of actions—iteratively refining grasp strategies until they achieve precision and reliability. This capability finds applications in fields ranging from warehouse logistics to healthcare, where robots handle delicate medical instruments.

The world of gaming stands as a playground where reinforcement learning's potential shines. Gaming environments offer the perfect arena for agents to learn and evolve strategies through interactions. From classic board games to contemporary video games, reinforcement learning transcends the confines of scripted opponents, fostering adaptive adversaries that challenge players.

Consider chess—a domain where Deep Blue's victory over a grandmaster marked a milestone in AI. The evolution continues with reinforcement learning agents mastering games like Go and Dota 2. AlphaGo, powered by Q-Learning variants, defied human intuition to triumph in a game deemed too complex for brute-force calculations. In gaming, reinforcement learning's allure lies in its capacity to imbue virtual agents with strategies that evolve and adapt, enhancing player engagement and crafting richer, more dynamic experiences.

Autonomous systems, with self-driving vehicles at the forefront, epitomize the convergence of artificial intelligence and real-world impact. Reinforcement learning becomes a key enabler in navigating the complexities of real-world environments. For autonomous vehicles, learning through interactions with dynamic traffic, varied weather conditions, and unpredictable human behavior is paramount.

Reinforcement learning algorithms guide autonomous vehicles in learning safe and effective driving behaviors. These algorithms capture patterns from data generated during on-road testing, simulating millions of scenarios to train agents that adhere to traffic rules, anticipate hazards, and optimize fuel efficiency. The journey toward fully autonomous vehicles hinges on the capacity of reinforcement learning to simulate scenarios and expedite the learning curve.

Beyond driving, autonomous systems extend to aerial drones. Reinforcement learning equips drones with the ability to navigate unstructured environments, such as search and rescue missions or remote deliveries. Learning from simulated flights, drones optimize flight paths, adjust for wind currents, and avoid obstacles, ensuring efficient and safe navigation.

A common thread across these applications is the interplay between real-world interactions and simulated environments. Reinforcement learning leverages simulations to accelerate learning, explore possibilities, and refine strategies before transitioning to real-world scenarios. Simulations provide a controlled canvas where agents can learn without the constraints of risks or resource limitations.

In robotics, simulators recreate physical interactions, allowing robots to explore actions and reactions without tangible consequences. In gaming, agents engage in simulated battles, learning strategies before confronting players. In autonomous systems, simulations replicate driving conditions to train self-driving algorithms.

While the applications are promising, reinforcement learning confronts challenges inherent to the complexities of the real world. The exploration-exploitation trade-off persists as agents navigate uncertain terrains. Sparse rewards, common in real-world scenarios, can slow learning. Transfer learning—translating learned policies to new, untrained situations—remains a challenge as small variations demand significant adaptations.

The path forward weaves through hybrid approaches, safety measures, and improved transfer learning. Hybrid models that fuse reinforcement learning with imitation learning capitalize on the strengths of both paradigms. Safe reinforcement learning aims to mitigate risks associated with trial and error learning in real-world settings, ensuring that learning does not compromise safety.

In conclusion, reinforcement learning emerges as a beacon of transformation in robotics, gaming, and autonomous systems. It empowers robots with adaptability, crafts engaging gaming adversaries, and pioneers self-driving evolution. Through the synergy of algorithms and simulations, reinforcement learning bridges the gap between virtual exploration and real-world mastery.

As technology advances and challenges are surmounted, these applications will continue to evolve. Robotics will birth robots that master even more intricate tasks, gaming experiences will grow increasingly immersive, and autonomous systems will shape the landscape of transportation. Reinforcement learning, the thread that weaves through these realms, paves the way for a future where machines engage, adapt, and optimize decisions with profound finesse, enhancing human potential and reshaping the contours of innovation.

CHAPTER IX

Model Deployment and Scaling

Difficulties of deploying machine learning models in production

In the realm of machine learning, the journey from concept to deployment marks a transformative passage—a bridge between algorithmic innovation and real-world impact. As organizations harness the power of machine learning to drive decision-making and enhance processes, the challenges of deploying machine learning models in production emerge as formidable hurdles. This section embarks on an exploration of these challenges, delving into the intricacies that arise when translating models from the laboratory to the production environment. From data quality to performance monitoring, each challenge illuminates the complex landscape of deploying machine learning, uncovering the intricate dance between theory and practicality.

At the core of every successful machine learning model lies high-quality data—clean, consistent, and representative of the real-world scenarios the model will encounter. However, achieving pristine data is a formidable challenge. Real-world data often harbors imperfections, ranging from missing values and inconsistent formats to outliers and biases. These imperfections can lead to erroneous conclusions and suboptimal model performance when deployed.

Consider a model trained to predict customer preferences for an e-commerce platform. If the training data contains incomplete or inconsistent customer profiles, the deployed model may offer inaccurate recommendations, frustrating users and undermining trust. Addressing data quality requires a combination of data preprocessing, validation, and continuous monitoring, ensuring that the model's inputs remain reliable and the outputs remain trustworthy throughout the deployment lifecycle.

In the controlled environment of development, machine learning models often demonstrate impressive performance. However, the transition to production often reveals scalability challenges that arise when models face real-world demands. The demands of a single user during development pale in comparison to the thousands or millions of users concurrently accessing a deployed application.

Scalability challenges can manifest in slow response times, resource overutilization, and even system crashes. Imagine a recommendation system that slows to a crawl during peak shopping seasons, frustrating users and impacting sales. To navigate these challenges, organizations must architect their deployment infrastructure with scalability in mind, leveraging techniques such as load balancing, distributed computing, and cloud resources to ensure smooth and efficient model serving under varying workloads.

The journey of a machine learning model doesn't end with deployment—it's a continuum that demands ongoing vigilance. Models are like living organisms, subject to concept drift—the phenomenon where the statistical properties of the target variable change over time. This can result in a gradual decline in model performance, as the deployed model's assumptions become misaligned with real-world data.

Consider a fraud detection model deployed in a financial institution. Over time, the nature of fraudulent activities evolves, and if the model isn't regularly retrained or updated, it might miss new patterns of fraud, allowing illicit transactions to go undetected. This emphasize the importance of continuous monitoring and maintenance, involving periodic model updates, retraining on fresh data, and adapting to changing business dynamics. Machine learning deployment introduces ethical and fairness challenges that mirror societal concerns. Models trained on biased data can perpetuate and amplify biases, resulting in unfair decisions that disproportionately affect certain groups. This phenomenon is particularly alarming in domains like lending, hiring, and criminal justice. Imagine an algorithm used in a hiring platform that inadvertently discriminates against candidates from certain demographics due to historical biases in training data. Deploying such a model not only reinforces inequality but also exposes organizations to legal and reputational risks. Addressing ethical and fairness concerns demands rigorous data curation, thorough bias analysis, and the incorporation of fairness-enhancing techniques into the model development pipeline.

Deploying machine learning models introduces security and privacy challenges that echo the broader landscape of cybersecurity. Models, like software, can be vulnerable to attacks—adversaries might attempt to manipulate inputs to produce unintended outputs, leading to undesirable consequences. Furthermore, models trained on sensitive data can inadvertently leak private information, compromising user privacy.

Consider a medical diagnosis model deployed in a healthcare institution. If an attacker manipulates input data to trigger a misdiagnosis, patient safety could be compromised. Addressing security concerns demands robust testing, input validation, and adversarial training to fortify models against attacks. For privacy, techniques like differential privacy and secure multi-party computation can shield sensitive data from exposure.

Even the most accurate machine learning model can fall short if it doesn't align with user expectations and needs. The challenge of user experience emerges as a pivotal consideration in deployment. Models that generate recommendations, translations, or responses should feel natural, coherent, and aligned with user preferences. Consider a language translation model deployed in a chat application. If the translations it produces are overly formal or lack contextual fluency, users might find the conversation stilted and unnatural. Designing machine learning models for optimal user experience requires a blend of technological prowess and human-centered design, involving user feedback, interface design, and careful crafting of model outputs.

In conclusion, the odyssey of deploying machine learning models in production embodies a complex interplay of challenges that span data, scalability, monitoring, ethics, security, and user-centricity. Each challenge represents a puzzle to solve, a path to navigate, and an opportunity to bridge the gap between theoretical innovation and real-world impact. Successful deployment requires a holistic approach that transcends algorithms, embracing data stewardship, infrastructure engineering, ethics, and user-centric design.

As the deployment landscape evolves, organizations must be agile and adaptive, prepared to learn from failures and iterate toward success. Addressing these challenges is not merely a technical endeavor—it's a commitment to ethical responsibility, user trust, and the transformative potential of machine learning in the real world. With every challenge overcome, the landscape of deploying machine learning models transforms from a maze into a path, guided by innovation, resilience, and the pursuit of a smarter, more impactful future.

Discussion of containerization, microservices, and serverless architecture for scalable deployment

In the realm of technology, the ability to scale effectively is the cornerstone of success, especially in a world driven by data and user demands. As organizations strive to meet ever-increasing computational needs, the architectural paradigms of containerization, microservices, and serverless architecture have emerged as powerful tools for achieving scalable deployment. This section embarks on a journey to explore these paradigms, delving into their mechanics, strengths, and real-world applications. From streamlining development to optimizing resource utilization, each paradigm illuminates the intricate dance between architecture and scalability, carving pathways toward a more agile and responsive technological landscape.

Containerization, epitomized by technologies like Docker, introduces a level of abstraction that simplifies the deployment process while enhancing consistency across diverse environments. Containers encapsulate an application along with its dependencies and runtime libraries, creating portable units that can run consistently across different platforms—be it development, testing, or production.

Consider an e-commerce application that performs seamlessly during testing but faces compatibility issues when deployed on a production server. Containerization addresses this challenge by packaging the application, its code, and the necessary libraries into a self-contained unit. This eliminates the "it works on my machine" syndrome and ensures that the application behaves consistently across different stages of the development pipeline.

Furthermore, containerization enhances scalability by allowing organizations to scale up or down efficiently. When the demand surges, multiple instances of containers can be launched, creating a swarm of identical units that share the application's load. Container orchestration tools like Kubernetes automate this process, seamlessly handling the distribution and management of containers across clusters of machines. Microservices architecture advocates breaking down applications into smaller, loosely coupled services that can be created, deployed, and scaled independently. This approach contrasts with monolithic architecture, where the entire application resides in a single codebase, making it challenging to update or scale specific components without affecting the entire system.

Imagine a large e-commerce platform where even minor changes require redeploying the entire application, causing downtime and disruption. Microservices address this by allowing developers to focus on individual services, making updates and enhancements more agile. For instance, a payment gateway service can be scaled independently to handle peak shopping seasons, ensuring smooth transactions without impacting other services.

Microservices enhance scalability by distributing workloads and optimizing resource allocation. Individual services can be scaled depending on their specific demands, enabling organizations to allocate resources precisely where they are needed. This granular approach minimizes wastage of resources and maximizes efficiency.

Serverless architecture reimagines the way applications are deployed, focusing on the execution of functions in response to events. In this paradigm, developers write functions that perform specific tasks, and the cloud provider handles the underlying infrastructure, automatically scaling resources as needed.

Consider a photo-sharing application that generates thumbnails for uploaded images. In a traditional setup, maintaining servers to handle varying image processing demands can be resource-intensive and complex. Serverless architecture addresses this by allowing developers to write a thumbnail-generation function, which automatically scales based on the number of image uploads, without requiring manual intervention.

Serverless architecture optimizes resource utilization by charging organizations only for the actual compute resources used during the execution of functions. This "pay as you go" model aligns with actual demand, making it cost-effective and efficient, especially for applications with variable workloads.

The strength of these paradigms isn't confined to isolation; they often complement and enhance each other in a hybrid approach. For instance, organizations can containerize individual microservices, leveraging the agility of microservices architecture while benefiting from the consistency and portability of containerization.

Consider an online gaming platform where different microservices handle player authentication, game logic, and leaderboards. Containerization of these microservices ensures that they can be easily deployed across different environments. Kubernetes orchestration enhances scalability by efficiently managing container clusters, dynamically allocating resources to handle varying player loads.
Serverless architecture can further complement this hybrid approach. For example, a gaming platform may use serverless functions to handle real-time analytics, generating insights on player behavior. These functions, triggered by events such as player actions or game sessions, provide an elastic compute layer that seamlessly integrates with the containerized microservices, optimizing the overall architecture for agility and scalability.

The power of these architectural paradigms is showcased across diverse real-world applications. Airbnb, for instance, leverages microservices architecture to enhance its booking and reservation system. Each service, containerized for consistency, can be scaled individually to manage varying booking demands, ensuring a seamless experience for users.

Netflix, a pioneer in cloud-native architecture, utilizes a hybrid approach that combines microservices and containerization. The streaming giant employs serverless architecture to optimize transcoding tasks, where videos are converted into different formats. This offloads compute-intensive workloads, freeing up resources for other microservices that power the user experience.

While these architectural paradigms hold transformative potential, they also confront challenges reflective of their complexity. Containerization requires careful orchestration to manage clusters effectively, avoiding over-provisioning or resource bottlenecks. Microservices demand robust communication mechanisms to ensure seamless interactions among different services. Serverless architecture, while agile, introduces latency due to the time required to initialize and execute functions.

The path forward lies in refining these paradigms and addressing their limitations. Continuous advancements in container orchestration, service discovery, and network management contribute to efficient containerization. Microservices can benefit from evolving communication protocols and automated testing frameworks to maintain coherence. Serverless platforms are continuously optimizing execution speed and minimizing cold start latency to ensure a responsive experience.

In conclusion, containerization, microservices, and serverless architecture collectively shape the future of scalable deployment. They embody the evolution of technology, from rigid monoliths to agile, dynamic units of compute. These paradigms empower organizations to build, deploy, and scale applications efficiently, embracing the evolving demands of data-driven enterprises and user-centric experiences.

As organizations chart their technological journey, they must navigate the intricacies of these paradigms, striking the right balance between their strengths and limitations. The hybrid landscape emerges as a testament to the adaptability of technology—a space where paradigms intertwine, complement, and amplify each other.

In the dynamic realm of technology, the scalable future beckons—a landscape where containerized microservices orchestrate serverless functions, responding to real-world events with agility. This future, built on the pillars of containerization, microservices, and serverless architecture, promises not just scalable deployment but also a technological evolution that adapts and thrives in the face of complexity, variability, and the uncharted horizons of innovation.

Considerations for monitoring, maintenance, and updating of deployed models

In the constantly changing landscape of artificial intelligence, the journey doesn't end with model deployment; in many ways, it's just the beginning. Deployed models, once heralded for their potential, must be nurtured and tended with care to ensure they continue to deliver accurate insights, intelligent actions, and impactful results. The considerations of monitoring, maintenance, and updating are at the core of this stewardship, forming the bedrock upon which reliable, resilient, and effective AI systems are built. This section embarks on a voyage through these considerations, unveiling the intricacies of model care, the challenges of sustaining performance, and the strategies that organizations employ to traverse the evolving terrain of AI deployment.

Monitoring, akin to a vigilant guardian, plays a pivotal role in ensuring the sustained health and effectiveness of deployed models. Monitoring encompasses a spectrum of activities—ranging from tracking model performance to capturing anomalous behavior and identifying degradation over time. It is the lens through which organizations gain insights into how models interact with real-world data and make informed decisions.

Consider a fraud detection system deployed in a financial institution. Effective monitoring ensures that the system accurately detects fraudulent transactions, minimizing financial losses. Regularly tracking metrics like precision, recall, and false positives enables organizations to intervene when model performance deviates from expectations, thereby preserving the system's integrity.

Continuous monitoring is particularly critical in dynamic environments where data distributions shift, user behaviors evolve, and external factors influence model outcomes. Adaptive monitoring strategies, bolstered by automated alert systems, provide organizations with timely notifications, enabling proactive interventions to correct performance dips or address emerging issues. The

journey of a deployed model is akin to maintaining a fine-tuned instrument—the harmonious chords of accurate predictions and valuable insights require ongoing care. Model maintenance involves the careful management of changing data distributions, evolving business goals, and the incessant march of technological advancements.

In a scenario where a recommendation system is deployed for an e-commerce platform, maintenance is essential to address evolving customer preferences, new product introductions, and shifting market trends. Frequent updates ensure that the recommendations remain relevant and aligned with user expectations.

Maintenance is also crucial to mitigate the risks of model decay, a phenomenon where model performance deteriorates as the real-world context evolves. Organizations must proactively retrain models on fresh data to capture changes, avoid bias accumulation, and adapt to new patterns.

Updating deployed models is a multidimensional art, requiring a delicate balance between agility and prudence. Model updates introduce the potential to enhance performance, fix issues, and integrate novel features. However, hasty updates can disrupt operations, introduce new problems, or alienate users accustomed to existing behavior.

Consider a voice recognition system deployed in a virtual assistant. An update aiming to improve recognition accuracy could inadvertently alter the system's behavior, leading to user frustration. Balancing innovation and stability is paramount, necessitating robust testing, staged rollouts, and mechanisms to revert to previous versions if issues arise.

Versioning plays a crucial role in model updating. It empowers organizations to iterate on models while preserving the ability to revert to prior versions. This practice also enables A/B testing, where multiple versions of a model are concurrently deployed to assess their impact before committing to a full rollout.

Ethics form a guiding compass when considering model updates and maintenance. As models evolve, the risk of unintended biases or fairness issues emerges. Model updates that inadvertently discriminate against certain demographic groups can perpetuate inequality, leading to ethical and legal implications.

For instance, consider a hiring platform that deploys a model to filter job applications. If the model is biased against candidates from specific backgrounds, updates that perpetuate this bias raise ethical concerns. Organizations must implement bias mitigation techniques, ongoing audits, and feedback loops to ensure that updates align with ethical standards.

To navigate the nuances of monitoring, maintenance, and updates, organizations adopt a holistic approach that combines technological prowess with organizational culture. A robust DevOps culture, focused on collaboration between development and operations teams, fosters effective model management. Version control systems as well as continuous integration/continuous deployment (or CI/CD) pipelines streamline the process of deploying updates.

Machine learning operations (MLOps) platforms offer a comprehensive toolkit for managing the entire lifecycle of deployed models. These platforms provide solutions for monitoring, versioning, automated testing, and staged rollouts, all while adhering to best practices for maintaining model health.

Regular communication between data scientists, engineers, domain experts, and end-users is crucial. It ensures that models remain aligned with business goals, user needs, and the evolving landscape.

In conclusion, monitoring, maintenance, and updating are the rhythmic cadence that propels the ongoing symphony of AI deployment. As organizations embark on the journey of model deployment, they must recognize that the ultimate measure of success lies not only in the initial impact but in the sustained excellence of the deployed systems. With the right strategies in place—effective

monitoring that guards against degradation, meticulous maintenance that ensures resilience, and judicious updates that balance innovation with stability—organizations can nurture AI solutions that evolve, adapt, and continue to deliver meaningful insights and actions in the ever-changing landscape of technology. The voyage of AI stewardship is an ongoing endeavor, a journey guided by the belief that the true potential of AI is realized not in creation alone but in the dedication to maintaining, nurturing, and enhancing its impact as it engages with the
world.

CHAPTER X

Ethical and Responsible AI

Ethical implications of advanced data science and machine learning

In the age of information, where data flows ceaselessly and algorithms wield unprecedented power, the ethical considerations surrounding advanced data science and machine learning have emerged as a compelling, complex, and indispensable discourse. As algorithms penetrate diverse facets of society—guiding decisions, shaping opinions, and influencing behaviors—the implications ripple across domains, ranging from privacy and bias to accountability and transparency. This section embarks on an exploration of these ethical implications, delving into the moral contours that underpin the deployment of advanced data science and machine learning. From the subtle biases embedded in algorithms to the quest for algorithmic accountability, each ethical facet uncovers the intricacies of this multidimensional landscape and resonates with the ethical compass that must guide the evolution of AI in a responsible, equitable, and just manner.

While algorithms promise objectivity, they often inherit the biases present in their training data, perpetuating systemic inequalities and unjust decisions. Consider a hiring algorithm that perpetuates gender bias, inadvertently favoring male candidates due to historical imbalances in the training data. Such bias not only reinforces discrimination but also hampers diversity and perpetuates a cycle of inequality.

To address algorithmic bias, a multifaceted approach is essential. Data preprocessing techniques that mitigate bias, diverse and representative training data, and thorough audits to identify discriminatory patterns can help counteract biases embedded in algorithms. Transparency in model design and decision-making processes is paramount, enabling external scrutiny and accountability.

As data becomes more pervasive, preserving individual privacy takes center stage. Advanced data science often entails collecting, analyzing, and sharing vast amounts of personal information, raising concerns about surveillance, tracking, and potential misuse. Consider location-based apps that continuously collect user data, potentially compromising user privacy and security.

Ethical data practices demand anonymization, data encryption, and clear consent mechanisms to ensure that individuals retain control over their data. Organizations must strike a delicate balance between deriving insights from data and safeguarding individual rights, reinforcing the ethical imperative to prioritize privacy and data protection.

The opacity of some advanced algorithms—often referred to as "black box" models—can raise ethical concerns. When algorithms make consequential decisions, their inner workings become critical for accountability and understanding. Imagine a medical diagnosis algorithm that prescribes treatments without offering explanations. Lack of transparency in such cases can erode trust and hinder informed decision-making.

Opening the black box involves enhancing model interpretability. Techniques like feature visualization, attention mechanisms, and local explanation methods shed light on how models arrive at decisions. Greater transparency not only instills user confidence but also empowers developers to detect and correct biases, leading to more ethical and responsible AI deployment.

The ethical implications of data science and machine learning extend beyond individual algorithms to encompass broader accountability. When autonomous vehicles make life-or-death decisions, who bears responsibility in case of accidents? Or when recommendation systems inadvertently promote misinformation, who is accountable for the consequences?

To address accountability, a framework for assigning responsibility is essential. Regulatory guidelines, industry standards, and robust legal frameworks ensure that developers, organizations, and even AI itself are accountable for the consequences of algorithmic decisions. As algorithms become more autonomous, notions of accountability will need to evolve, encapsulating not just those who create the technology but those who deploy, use, and maintain it.

Equity and fairness emerge as central ethical considerations when algorithms influence access to resources, opportunities, and services. Algorithms, if biased, can perpetuate existing disparities and exacerbate social injustices. Consider a loan approval algorithm that disproportionately rejects applicants from historically marginalized communities due to biased training data.

Mitigating bias and ensuring fairness demand a conscious commitment. Fairness-aware algorithms, metrics that measure disparate impact, and the use of responsible AI practices during development are pivotal. This ethical journey requires confronting historical biases, fostering diversity in data collection and model development, and cultivating a culture of fairness.

Ethical implications necessitate a balance between innovation and safeguards. Algorithmic systems, left unchecked, can propagate misinformation, amplify extremist content, and manipulate opinions. As a result, the ethical discourse extends to the regulation of algorithms.

Regulation aims to ensure that algorithms adhere to ethical standards, transparency requirements, and legal guidelines. However, striking the right balance is challenging. Overregulation can stifle innovation, while underregulation can foster harm. Collaborative efforts among governments, industry players, and academia are essential to craft balanced regulations that foster innovation while safeguarding public interests.

As advanced data science and machine learning permeate the fabric of society, the ethical implications they introduce are both nuanced and far-reaching. The road ahead requires a concerted effort to navigate this ethical frontier, guided by principles of fairness, transparency, accountability, and empathy.

Addressing these ethical implications necessitates multidisciplinary collaboration. Ethicists, data scientists, policymakers, and domain experts must collectively design ethical AI systems that amplify societal benefits while mitigating harms. Initiatives like ethical AI guidelines, impact assessments, and ethical review boards are integral to aligning AI with human values.

Organizations must also adopt a culture of ethical responsibility. Training data scientists in ethical considerations, fostering diversity in AI teams, and empowering employees to raise ethical concerns contribute to a more ethical AI ecosystem.

The ethical implications of advanced data science and machine learning encapsulate the moral essence of our technological evolution. Each ethical facet—bias mitigation, privacy preservation, transparency, accountability, fairness, and regulation—forms a strand woven into the fabric of responsible AI deployment. The path forward is not without challenges, as ethical considerations intersect with technological innovation, regulatory frameworks, and societal norms. Yet, it is a journey imbued with ethical responsibility, one that embraces the potential of AI to enhance human lives while ensuring that its deployment remains just, equitable, and aligned with the values that define our shared humanity. In the labyrinth of advanced data science, the ethical compass stands as our guide, steering us toward a future where technology enriches rather than diminishes, uplifts rather than marginalizes, and reflects the best of our collective aspirations.

Discussion about bias, fairness, transparency, and accountability in AI systems

In the intricate tapestry of artificial intelligence (AI) systems, the threads of bias, fairness, transparency, and accountability are interwoven as foundational principles that shape not only the technology itself but also its profound impact on society. As AI applications pervade various domains—ranging from criminal justice and healthcare to finance and hiring—the ethical considerations associated with these principles come to the forefront. This section embarks on an in-depth discussion, unveiling the significance, challenges, and strategies surrounding bias mitigation, fairness enhancement, transparency promotion, and accountability assurance in AI systems. From recognizing the subtle biases encoded in data to fostering algorithmic systems that honor human values, each aspect unfolds as an ethical mandate that holds the key to the responsible advancement of AI technology.

As AI systems learn patterns from data, they inadvertently inherit biases present in that data, reflecting the biases of society itself. Imagine a predictive policing system trained on historical arrest data, which may perpetuate racial biases and result in discriminatory outcomes. Bias mitigation is the ethical imperative to identify and address these biases to ensure that AI systems do not reinforce inequities.
Mitigating bias begins with meticulous data curation. Data preprocessing techniques that adjust for imbalances, diversify training data, and incorporate fairness-enhancing strategies are integral. Regular bias audits, guided by metrics that quantify disparate impact, help uncover hidden biases. It's crucial to foster multidisciplinary collaborations involving domain experts, ethicists, and data scientists to scrutinize data for potential sources of bias.

Fairness amplifies the ethical impact of AI by striving to ensure that algorithms do not discriminate against any group based on protected attributes such as race, gender, or age. Yet, defining fairness in algorithms is multifaceted, as different fairness notions often conflict with one another. The challenge lies in balancing competing definitions and formulating a notion of fairness that aligns with societal values.

Consider a credit scoring model that unfairly denies loans to certain demographic groups. To enhance fairness, organizations can adopt fairness-aware machine learning techniques, which optimize models for fairness while preserving utility. These techniques aim to achieve proportional representation, equal opportunity, and other fairness objectives. However, fairness-enhancing strategies should be applied with care, considering trade-offs and the specific context of deployment.

The "black box" nature of some AI models—the inability to explain how decisions are made—raises ethical concerns about accountability, user trust, and unintended consequences. Transparency, or model interpretability, is the pursuit of unveiling the inner workings of algorithms to users, developers, and regulatory bodies alike. Opening the algorithmic black box involves the application of explainable AI (XAI) techniques. These include feature visualization, model-agnostic explanation methods, and rule-based models that provide insights into how an AI system arrives at decisions. Transparency not only fosters trust but also aids in identifying and rectifying biases or errors. As AI advances, researchers continue to explore innovative ways to enhance the interpretability of complex models.

Accountability in AI transcends the creators of algorithms, encompassing organizations, regulatory bodies, and even the algorithms themselves. With autonomous AI systems making decisions that affect human lives, accountability is essential to address potential harms, biases, and errors.

Consider an autonomous vehicle involved in an accident. Who is accountable—the manufacturer, the AI developer, or the user? Ensuring accountability necessitates regulatory frameworks that define responsibilities, liabilities, and the role of oversight bodies. In some cases, an "algorithmic bill of rights" can be established, outlining the rights and expectations users have when interacting with AI systems.

The journey toward responsible AI is fraught with ethical considerations and trade-offs. For instance, while enhancing transparency might increase user trust, it could also expose vulnerabilities and be exploited by malicious actors. Similarly, optimizing for fairness might unintentionally result in decreased predictive accuracy for certain groups.

Ethical considerations in AI require striking a delicate balance between competing principles. Organizations must engage in ethical decision-making that navigates these complexities. Engaging diverse stakeholders, embracing transparency in decision-making processes, and fostering open discussions about ethical dilemmas are essential to making informed choices.

As AI systems reshape industries, societies, and individual experiences, the ethical underpinnings of bias mitigation, fairness enhancement, transparency promotion, and accountability assurance emerge as the moral compass of the AI era. The journey to responsible AI demands the collective efforts of data scientists, ethicists, policymakers, and society at large.

Recognizing the bias inherent in data, organizations must commit to diligent data curation and deploy strategies that counteract systemic inequities. Pursuing fairness requires the application of fairness-aware techniques that strike equilibrium among competing notions. Transparency promotion involves opening the algorithmic black box, empowering users to understand, trust, and engage with AI systems. Ensuring accountability necessitates defining roles, responsibilities, and regulatory frameworks that encompass the AI ecosystem.

In the landscape of advanced data science and machine learning, ethical considerations stand as the bedrock of responsible innovation. By weaving these principles into the fabric of AI systems, we embrace a future where technology not only advances human capabilities but does so with a steadfast commitment to fairness, equity, and transparency. In the ethical tapestry of AI, each thread is a moral obligation, each consideration a commitment to the collective good—an imperative that guides the transformation of AI from a tool to a force for positive change.

Guidelines for developing responsible AI applications

In the quickly evolving landscape of artificial intelligence (AI), where innovation fuels progress and technology reshapes the contours of human existence, the concept of responsible AI emerges as a fundamental imperative. Developing AI applications that are not only powerful and efficient but also ethical and accountable requires a thoughtful and deliberate approach. This section embarks on a journey to unveil comprehensive guidelines for the development of responsible AI applications. From data collection and algorithm design to transparency and ongoing monitoring, each guideline illuminates the path toward harnessing AI's potential while safeguarding human values, equity, and societal well-being.

Ethical Data Collection

The foundation of responsible AI lies in the ethical collection of data. Data shapes AI models, influencing their outcomes and predictions. Organizations must prioritize data privacy, security, and consent throughout the data lifecycle. Data should be collected transparently, with clear communication about the purpose and use of data.

Guided by principles of informed consent and data minimization, developers should gather only the data necessary for the intended application. Anonymization and aggregation techniques can further protect individual identities. By ensuring that data collection respects human rights and legal standards, organizations lay the groundwork for ethical AI development.

Bias Mitigation

Inherent biases in data can inadvertently lead AI models to perpetuate unfair outcomes. Developers must meticulously identify, mitigate, and monitor bias in data and algorithms. A comprehensive understanding of the social context and potential sources of bias is crucial.

Guidelines for bias mitigation include diverse representation in training data, regular audits for biased patterns, and the use of fairness-aware algorithms. Ensuring that AI systems do not discriminate against any group fosters equity and promotes responsible AI deployment.

Transparent Algorithm Design

The opacity of AI algorithms poses ethical challenges, as users demand transparency and accountability.

Developers should strive for algorithmic transparency, allowing users to understand the rationale behind decisions made by AI systems.

Transparency can be achieved through model interpretability techniques such as explainable AI (XAI). Documentation detailing the algorithm's functioning, training data, and potential limitations fosters user trust. The ability to understand and challenge algorithmic decisions is pivotal to maintaining ethical integrity.

User Empowerment

Responsible AI applications empower users by providing them with control, understanding, and autonomy over AI-driven experiences. Developers must prioritize user consent, allowing users to make informed choices about how their data is used and what decisions AI systems can make on their behalf.

User-centric design ensures that AI applications enhance human capabilities without eroding dignity or agency. Incorporating user feedback loops, clear communication channels, and mechanisms to opt out of AI-driven interactions exemplify user empowerment and ethical AI deployment.

Accountability and Regulation

Developers and organizations must adhere to ethical codes and regulatory guidelines that shape the responsible development of AI applications. Regulatory frameworks should address the ethical implications of AI and set standards for accountability, transparency, and data protection.

Guidelines for accountability involve clear documentation of the AI application's development process, compliance with legal and ethical standards, and mechanisms for addressing user grievances. Ethical review boards and cross-disciplinary collaborations can provide oversight and ensure adherence to ethical principles.

Ongoing Monitoring and Adaptation

The journey of responsible AI doesn't end with deployment; it is an ongoing commitment. Developers should monitor AI applications to detect shifts in performance, bias, and ethical considerations over time. Regular audits, continuous data analysis, and engagement with stakeholders ensure that AI applications remain aligned with ethical standards and evolving societal norms. As AI systems interact with dynamic contexts, developers must be agile in adapting algorithms to preserve ethical integrity.

Collaboration and Transparency

Collaboration across disciplines, industries, and borders is essential for responsible AI development. Developers should engage ethicists, domain experts, legal professionals, and users throughout the development process.

Transparency in communication—about AI capabilities, limitations, and potential risks—fosters trust and accountability. Ethical considerations should be openly discussed, and mechanisms for users to report concerns or biases should be readily available.

Ethical Leadership

Leaders in AI organizations play a pivotal role in fostering ethical AI cultures. Ethical leadership emphasizes values such as fairness, accountability, and social responsibility.

Organizations should prioritize ethical training for employees, establish ethical guidelines, and ensure that the principles of responsible AI are woven into the fabric of the organization's mission and operations.
In conclusion, the guidelines for developing responsible AI applications set the course for a future where technology and ethics harmoniously coexist. As AI applications permeate diverse aspects of society, from healthcare and education to finance and entertainment, the ethical imperative becomes paramount. By adhering to ethical data collection, mitigating bias, promoting transparency, empowering users, ensuring accountability, monitoring AI applications, fostering collaboration, and embracing ethical leadership, developers embark on a journey that extends beyond innovation—it's a journey that shapes the narrative of AI's role in human progress.

In the landscape of AI development, responsible innovation isn't just a choice; it's an obligation to create technology that enhances human well-being, respects rights, and uplifts society. By adhering to these guidelines, developers assume the mantle of ethical stewardship, paving the way for AI applications that amplify human potential while honoring human values. In this convergence of technology and ethics, the future is not only advanced but also compassionate, not only efficient but also equitable—a future where AI applications reflect the best of humanity's aspirations and potential.

CONCLUSION

Summary of the key takeaways covered in the e-book

In the field of the digital realm, where data weaves narratives of insights and algorithms orchestrate symphonies of intelligence, this e-book has ventured to explore the intricate dimensions of "Data Science and Machine Learning Demystified: Mastering Data Science and Machine Learning- Advanced Techniques and Applications." As we draw the curtains on this journey, it's fitting to reflect upon the key points and transformative insights that have unfolded across the chapters. From laying the foundation in data preprocessing to soaring into the realms of advanced machine learning algorithms, deep learning, NLP, computer vision, time series analysis, reinforcement learning, ethical considerations, and responsible AI development, this summary encapsulates the mosaic of knowledge that has illuminated our path.

The e-book embarked with an introduction to the exhilarating landscape of data science and machine learning. It emphasized that while algorithms and techniques are integral, understanding the data's context and domain is the cornerstone of success. The stages of the data science pipeline, including data collection, preprocessing, exploration, modeling, evaluation, and deployment, provide a holistic framework for deriving actionable insights from raw data.

Data preprocessing emerged as the vital bridge between raw data and meaningful insights. Techniques such as handling missing data, outlier detection, and feature scaling were explored in depth. It became clear that data quality is paramount, as the quality of insights is directly proportional to the quality of the input data. Through diligent preprocessing, we pave the way for models that capture the true essence of the domain.

The exploration extended to advanced preprocessing techniques, with a focus on dimensionality reduction. Techniques like Principal Component Analysis (or PCA) and t-Distributed Stochastic Neighbor Embedding (or t-SNE) unveiled the art of reducing data's complexity while retaining its essence. By compressing data into lower dimensions, we gain efficiency and facilitate the interpretation of high-dimensional data.

With the foundation in place, the e-book delved into the realm of advanced machine learning algorithms. Gradient Boosting, Random Forest, as well as Support Vector Machines (SVM) emerged as powerful tools that transcend the limitations of basic models. These algorithms embrace ensemble methods, model stacking, and non-linear decision boundaries, enabling us to tackle complex tasks with enhanced accuracy and robustness.

Neural networks became the focal point as the e-book transitioned into deep learning—a paradigm that has revolutionized AI. The structure of neural networks, with layers of interconnected nodes, mimics the human brain's structure. Deep learning thrives on data and leverages hierarchical feature extraction to deliver state-of-the-art performance in tasks like image recognition, natural language processing (or NLP), and more.

The e-book charted the applications of deep learning across diverse domains. In computer vision, Convolutional Neural Networks (CNNs) excel in image analysis, detecting patterns and objects within visual data. In the realm of natural language processing (or

NLP), Recurrent Neural Networks (or RNNs) and Long Short-Term Memory (or LSTM) networks unravel the complexities of language, while Transformers have redefined how we process sequential data.

Two prominent frameworks—TensorFlow and PyTorch—illuminated the path toward practical implementation. TensorFlow's flexibility and scalability cater to diverse applications, while PyTorch's dynamic computation graph empowers developers with a more intuitive and exploratory development experience. These frameworks democratize deep learning, making it accessible to researchers, engineers, and enthusiasts alike.

Natural Language Processing (NLP) emerged as a captivating discipline that bridges the gap between human language and computational analysis. Its significance lies in its applications, from sentiment analysis to named entity recognition, machine translation, and beyond. Pre-trained language models like BERT and GPT-3 have revolutionized NLP, enabling systems to understand, generate, and interact with human language at remarkable levels of sophistication.

Computer vision brought the world of images into focus. From object detection, where algorithms identify and locate objects within images, to image segmentation that divides images into meaningful regions, computer vision paves the way for autonomous vehicles, medical diagnostics, and surveillance systems that augment human capabilities.

The artistry of computer vision extended to image generation, where Generative Adversarial Networks (GANs) harnessed the power of adversarial training to create realistic images. GANs' generative prowess birthed applications in art, fashion, and even the generation of hyper-realistic deepfakes, underscoring the dual nature of AI's creative potential.

Time series data, often characterized by temporal dependencies, emerged as a distinct challenge and opportunity. From stock market predictions and weather forecasting to healthcare monitoring and industrial maintenance, time series analysis forms the bedrock of informed decision-making in domains where time matters.

In the realm of time series analysis, advanced techniques like Autoregressive Integrated Moving Average (ARIMA), Long Short-Term Memory (LSTM) networks, and Facebook's Prophet emerged as stalwarts. ARIMA captures patterns in stationary time series, LSTM networks model long-term dependencies, and Prophet forecasts with a focus on seasonality and trend.

The e-book traversed through time series applications, unveiling their significance across sectors. In finance, time series models drive investment decisions and risk management. In healthcare, they forecast disease outbreaks and inform patient care. The applications underscored the universal nature of time series analysis, transcending disciplines and industries.

The journey extended into unsupervised learning, a realm where AI seeks patterns without explicit labels. Clustering techniques like k-means, hierarchical clustering, and DBSCAN grouped similar data points, while anomaly detection identified rare and unusual instances—an approach critical to fraud detection and industrial fault diagnosis.

The realm of unsupervised learning found its applications in diverse scenarios. In customer segmentation, clustering techniques carved segments based on behavior and preferences. Anomaly detection flagged unusual behaviors or events, aiding cybersecurity, fraud detection, and equipment maintenance.

Reinforcement learning unfolded as a paradigm where AI agents learn from their interactions with an environment. Guided by rewards and penalties, these agents make sequential decisions that span from gaming strategies to robotics, finance, and self-driving cars.

Reinforcement learning's potential echoed across applications. In robotics, it steered agile maneuvers and complex tasks. In gaming, it played strategic games with unparalleled precision. In autonomous systems, it navigated through uncertain terrains and environments.

Ethics emerged as the ethical underpinning of AI's evolution. The significance of addressing bias, fairness, transparency, and accountability in AI systems paved the way for responsible AI deployment. Developers should navigate the complex terrain, ensuring that AI systems enhance human dignity, uphold human rights, and mitigate harm.

The journey culminated with guidelines for responsible AI development. Ethical data collection, bias mitigation, transparency promotion, user empowerment, accountability assurance, ongoing monitoring, collaboration, and ethical leadership form the pillars of AI development that respects human values and aligns with societal needs.

As we conclude this journey, the tapestry of knowledge woven across the chapters resonates as a testament to the power of data science and machine learning. From understanding the nuances of data preprocessing to embracing the potentials of deep learning, NLP, computer vision, time series analysis, and responsible AI development, this e-book has uncovered the multidimensional realm where AI intersects with human ingenuity.

In this synthesis of insights, we are reminded that AI is not merely a technological marvel; it's a reflection of human endeavor, curiosity, and aspiration. The chapters, like interlocking puzzle pieces, have constructed a panoramic view of AI's potential and the ethical considerations that accompany it. With each layer of knowledge peeled back, we find not only answers but also the impetus to ask the right questions—questions that guide us toward ethical innovation, societal progress, and a future enriched by the harmonious fusion of human and artificial intelligence.

The significance of continuous learning as well as staying updated in the rapidly evolving field of data science and machine learning

In the digital age, where information travels at the speed of light and technology reshapes the landscape with each passing moment, the realm of data science and machine learning is a testament to the boundless potential of human ingenuity. In this intricate tapestry of algorithms and insights, the significance of continuous learning as well as staying updated emerges as an unwavering beacon—a navigational star that guides practitioners through the ever-evolving seas of knowledge. This section embarks on a voyage to unveil the profound significance of continuous learning in the rapidly changing field of data science and machine learning. From the rapid pace of technological advancement to the transformative potential of lifelong learning, we explore how staying updated transcends being a necessity to becoming a fundamental pillar of success and innovation.

In the digital realm, change is the only constant. The field of data science and machine learning exemplifies this reality with unparalleled clarity. The algorithms that drive today's innovations can become obsolete tomorrow as new techniques emerge, and paradigms shift. Machine learning models that were cutting-edge a year ago might now be eclipsed by more sophisticated architectures. The tools and frameworks that once dominated the landscape can be dethroned by newer, more efficient alternatives.

Consider the realm of natural language processing (NLP), where the advent of transformer-based models like BERT and GPT-3 has transformed language understanding and generation. In computer vision, the progression from traditional feature extraction methods to convolutional neural networks (CNNs) redefined image analysis. Such shifts are not isolated events; they are emblematic of the rapid evolution that characterizes the data science and machine learning landscape.

In this environment of perpetual change, the concept of lifelong learning emerges as a potent antidote. It's not enough to possess knowledge—the ability to acquire new skills and adapt to novel paradigms defines the edge between stagnation and progress. Lifelong learning transcends formal education, emphasizing the continuous acquisition of knowledge through self-directed exploration, courses, workshops, and engaging with a vibrant community of practitioners.

Lifelong learning nurtures expertise by cultivating a growth mindset—an approach that sees challenges as opportunities for learning and views failure as a stepping stone toward improvement. This mindset is essential in the data science and machine learning landscape, where the uncharted territories of new algorithms, frameworks, and techniques demand adaptability and a willingness to embrace the unknown.

In a competitive landscape where organizations vie for innovation and professionals strive for career advancement, staying updated emerges as a formidable competitive edge. The ability to harness the latest tools, leverage cutting-edge techniques, and interpret emerging trends positions individuals as thought leaders and practitioners at the forefront of progress.

Consider the explosion of AI ethics and responsible AI practices. As the ethical implications of AI technologies gain prominence, professionals who are well-versed in bias mitigation, fairness-aware algorithms, and transparent AI design are uniquely equipped to address societal concerns and guide organizations toward ethical innovation.

The field's dynamism calls for adaptability—a trait that continuous learning fosters. As AI technologies evolve, new challenges emerge. Take, for instance, the ethical considerations surrounding AI deployment. The landscape has evolved from a focus on algorithms to encompassing bias mitigation, transparency, and accountability. Professionals who continually educate themselves on these evolving concerns are poised to navigate ambiguity and pioneer solutions that align with societal values.

Adaptation is also pivotal in harnessing opportunities. The rise of AI in healthcare, for example, demands professionals who understand both the medical domain and the latest AI techniques. By staying updated, experts can bridge the gap between innovation and application, creating solutions that revolutionize patient care.

Innovation is the heart of data science and machine learning. By staying updated, professionals fuel innovation by incorporating novel ideas into their projects. Consider the advances in deep learning, which have led to breakthroughs in image recognition, speech synthesis, and language understanding. Innovations like these arise when practitioners fuse new techniques with domain knowledge, pioneering solutions that reshape industries.

Moreover, the interdisciplinary nature of data science and machine learning underscores the importance of diverse knowledge. Professionals who continually explore new domains, from neuroscience to economics, can introduce unconventional perspectives that inspire creative solutions to complex problems.

The pursuit of continuous learning is not a solitary endeavor—it thrives in the ecosystem of collaboration. Data science and machine learning community is a global network of learners who share insights, discoveries, and challenges. Online forums, conferences, and workshops provide platforms for practitioners to engage with peers, exchange ideas, and collectively push the boundaries of knowledge.

Collaboration also catalyzes the adoption of emerging techniques. When professionals come together to explore a new algorithm or framework, their combined expertise accelerates understanding and adoption, propelling the field forward.

As we navigate the labyrinthine landscapes of data science and machine learning, we are reminded that the journey is unbounded by time. The pursuit of continuous learning is not a destination—it's a perpetual expedition that transcends roles, industries, and technological paradigms. In a field where algorithms can become antiquated in the blink of an eye, and insights transform into innovation with each breakthrough, the importance of staying updated becomes an indomitable force.

Lifelong learning is not a burden; it's an opportunity—a passage to remain relevant, impactful, and at the vanguard of progress. As technology propels us into the future, let us embrace the ethos of continuous learning—a journey that celebrates curiosity, fosters innovation, and ensures that we remain unceasingly equipped to unravel the mysteries of data, the potential of algorithms, and the infinite tapestry of possibilities that data science and machine learning promise to unfold.

Thank you for buying and reading/listening to our book. If you found this book useful/helpful please take a few minutes and leave a review on the platform where you purchased our book. Your feedback matters greatly to us.

www.ingramcontent.com/pod-product-compliance
Lightning Source LLC
Chambersburg PA
CBHW071512150726
48000CB00002B/560